GEORGE FREDERICK MACLEAR. D.D.

BORN 3 FEBRUARY 1833.
DIED 19 OCTOBER 1902.

Lectures

ON

Pastoral Theology

BY THE LATE

REVEREND G. F. MACLEAR. D.D.

Warden of St. Augustine's College, Canterbury.

EDITED BY

THE REVEREND R. J. E. BOGGIS. B.D.

Sub-Warden of St. Augustine's College, Canterbury.

Canterbury:
CROSS & JACKMAN.

Milwaukee:
THE YOUNG CHURCHMAN CO.
1904.

40793

DEDICATION.

The writer of these Lectures, the Reverend Dr. George Frederick Maclear, who for twenty-two years was Warden of St. Augustine's Missionary College at Canterbury, left behind him at his death a considerable store of manuscripts —chiefly courses of lectures that he had delivered to the Students of St. Augustine's, or sermons preached in the College Chapel or elsewhere; and the editor of this little volume is of opinion that such a wealth of material, penned by so well-known and so influential a teacher and preacher, ought not to be allowed to perish. He has therefore taken in hand the task of presenting to the general reader a small portion of these literary remains, hoping to be able to judge by the result whether it would be advisable to publish more at a future time.

Dr. Maclear's name is so well and so widely known throughout the Anglican world, that it is not necessary to describe the enormous service that he has rendered to the Church. Suffice it to say that of his thirty published works— of which over 850,000 volumes have been sold—the best known are his theological manuals on the Old Testament, the New Testament, the Church Catechism, the Creeds, and the Articles; and he also gained a large circulation for his books on missionary topics—the *Apostles of Mediæval Europe,* and the *Conversion of the Celts, the Englishmen, the Northmen, and the Slavs.* Some of these have been adopted as standards of teaching in the majority of the higher grade schools and colleges of the British Isles, and have similarly found favour in the Colonies, and some have been translated into several foreign languages. Thus educationalists and theological students are familiar with his reputation as an author wherever the Church of England is to be found.

His experience of clerical life and work was a varied one. A country curacy at Clophill in Bedfordshire, town curacies at Lambeth and Mayfair and Notting Hill, an Assistant Preachership at the Temple Church, the Head-mastership of King's College School, London, and finally the long occupancy of the Wardenship of St. Augustine's —all this, added to his diligence as a student and his ability as a writer of vigorous English, made him well qualified to deal with such a subject as Pastoral Theology. And further, we may add, there are probably few priests in England, even among the parochial clergy, who have exercised the " ministry of preaching " so constantly and methodically as he.

The characteristics of the man and of his teaching were skilfully portrayed in the *In Memoriam* article of the *Guardian* of October 22nd, 1902. "Dr. Maclear combined in a very remarkable degree three characteristics not often found in the same man: he was a born teacher, an indefatigable worker, and a really sympathetic priest. That he was a born teacher every one who came in contact with him realized at once. Teaching was his great delight ; he was never so happy as when he was taking a class, or conducting a *vivâ voce* examination, or lecturing. Teaching was in him nothing less than a passion, his aptitude for it almost amounting to a form of genius. Perspicuity—clearness—was what he impressed on all his pupils. He had a positive love for looking over papers which were shown up neatly, and in which the writing was clear, the paragraphs distinctly marked, and the subject matter uninvolved. His deafness hindered him much in later years in this work of teaching, but his eye-sight was of the very best, and he could almost see what a man said if he did not hear it. He was an indefatigable worker; the work that he did when Head-master of King's College School was by no means confined to the school, as his numerous books and sermons testify; and when he left London he was told by the doctors that he ought to work less hard, and it was in the hope that he would be able to carry out this direction that he came to Canterbury in 1880. He soon found, however, that the work required of him there was not less, but even more than he had been doing at King's. The incessant correspondence, partly caused by the difficulty of raising funds for the students' fees, the number of subjects in which he was obliged to lecture, and the exacting nature of the college routine—all these told upon him as the years went by. But it is doubted whether he could ever really take a rest. The present writer has known him lecture for three or even four con-secutive hours day after day without feeling any strain. On Saturdays at St. Augustine's, which used to be free from lectures, the Warden took to giving lectures on Church History and other subjects to anyone who liked to come from the town; and these lectures were, for a number of years, largely attended and very deeply appreciated. On Sundays he was never idle. He celebrated early in the college chapel, and generally preached at mid-day, while in the evening he was almost sure to be preaching at one of the churches in Canterbury or at a village a few miles away. A born teacher and an indefatigable worker, he would often put young men to shame. But this was only one, though the most obvious, side of his character; he had also the heart of a priest. Thoroughly apprehending, as he did, the sacramental side of Church teaching, he was ready always to help anyone by hearing his confession or in other less formal ways. There must be scores of men all over the world now who not only got their first insight or a deeper insight into theology from the Warden, but who learnt from him how to hate sin and love God; how to take pains with their own character—to be careful about their self-examination, their prayers and meditations, and their communions. He had a very tender heart, and no one who went to him in any trouble could fail to come away without being braced and strengthened by his kind encouragement and true-hearted sympathy."

It is hoped that the publication of these lectures will help to extend and deepen the influence of a great teacher; and that to many former Students of St. Augustine's, who in years past sat at the feet of this their Gamaliel, and are now scattered abroad in far distant climes, this little volume will recall the features of one whom they venerated, and will revive happy memories of how in days that are gone they watched him pacing across the court of their beloved College, or listened to his familiar voice delivering (it may be) these very lectures in the Museum, or in the Chapel felt his hand resting upon their heads as they knelt before the altar. There are many such Augustinians to be found, who have gone forth from these walls and are doing the Master's work in many a foreign land, and to these especially this book is dedicated.

St. Augustine's College,
    Canterbury.

March 1904.

CHAPTER I.

INTRODUCTION.

The term Pastoral Theology may be defined as being "the practical application of the truths of Theology to the ministry of souls." Till the Redeemer of mankind came, the idea of the consecration of a vast body of men to the Pastoral oversight of others in respect to their spiritual interests may be said to have been more or less wholly unknown. Judaism had its priests and prophets; Heathen religions had their soothsayers and sorcerers. But the conception of a great Ministry, to which, in the true sense of the word, the Pastoral character could be applied, had not dawned upon the minds of men, or been conceived by any religious teachers.

The voice of Jewish prophecy, indeed, had described the coming of One, Who should feed His flock like a shepherd, and gather the lambs in His arms, and carry them in His bosom.* But till our Lord appeared incarnate, the outline sketched by the prophet had not been filled up. At length, in the fulness of time, He deigned out of the infinity of His love

*Isai. xl. 11; Ezek. xxxiv. 12; Zech. xi. 15, 16.

A

to unite our human nature in an indissoluble union with His Divine Nature, and to proclaim Himself "the Good Shepherd,"* Who had come to reclaim the lost sheep of fallen humanity.

Ever since the day when He uttered these words, and gave them substance and reality by His life of humiliation and His death upon the Cross, the Pastoral figure has ever been associated with His Person and His work. Hence writing some forty years after the Ascension, St. Peter, to whom the command had been given " to feed His sheep and tend His lambs,"† calls Him "the Shepherd of souls "‡ and "the chief Shepherd,"§ and the writer of the Epistle to the Hebrews entitles Him " the great shepherd of the sheep."‖ And so when the stress of persecution drove the faithful to take refuge in the catacombs of Rome, burrowed out beneath the streets of the Pagan City, the figure of the Good Shepherd was above all others most commonly sketched in rude outline on the walls of their dark prison-houses.

The true conception, therefore, of the Pastoral Office must be grounded on its complete realization in the personal work of the Good Shepherd. "It was said," we are told, "by a devoted layman of our Communion on his deathbed,

---

* Ὁ ποιμὴν ὁ καλός, John x. 11, 14.

† John xxi. 15, 16.   ‡ I Peter ii. 25.   § I Peter v. 4.

‖ Heb. xiii. 20.   The word " Pastor " occurs in the first Ember Collect—
" At this time so guide and govern the minds of Thy servants the Bishops and Pastors of Thy flock "; in the Collect for St. Matthias' Day—" may be ordered and guided by faithful and true Pastors"; and in the opening Prayer at the Consecration of Bishops—" Give grace to all Bishops, the Pastors of Thy Church."

that reviewing his life, the omission which he chiefly
deplored was that he had not made a daily effort
to study and imitate our Lord as described in the
Gospels."* But if this was the confession of a layman, how far more often might it be made by those,
whose special office it is to carry on that Ministry,
which He first began amongst men ! Whatever others
may say, they, whom by His Providence He calls
to represent Him to men as " Shepherds of souls,"
and "to seek for His sheep that are dispersed abroad,
and for His children who are in the midst of this
naughty world, that they may be saved through Him
for ever,"† cannot refuse to listen to His words,
where He says, "If any man serve Me, let him
follow Me." They at any rate are pre-eminently
bound to follow Him, and to endeavour themselves
to walk in the "footsteps of His most Holy life."

*Liddon's *Easter Sermons in St. Paul's*, vol. ii., p. 192. The *Imitatio Christi* of the great Flemish recluse was the favourite book of such opposite characters as General Gordon and George Eliot.

† *See* the Ordination Service for Priests.

CHAPTER II.

OUR LORD'S THIRTY YEARS OF PATIENT PREPARATION.

Considering the unique character of our Lord's Mission and its utter unlikeness to anything the world had ever seen before, we might have expected to be told much of His boyhood and early years. Instead of this, one or two verses cover the whole period of His preparation for His Ministry.

In the true Gospels we hear nothing of those premature exhibitions of miraculous power, which abound in the Apocryphal Gospels. He, who was perfect Man as well as perfect God, made "gradual progress" from infancy to boyhood, from boyhood to youth, and from youth to manhood.* He hurried nothing: He anticipated nothing. All was natural and therefore all was Divine.

Nazareth, where our Lord grew in wisdom and stature, was no place which might have attracted the eastern sage or the western recluse. It was in the very centre of the activity of Galilee of

* Προέκοπτε. Luke ii. 52.

the Gentiles, and was unknown and unnamed in the
Old Testament. The home of Joseph and Mary
presented, we may believe, nothing in its external
features to distinguish it from other homes at
Nazareth. What Lancashire and Yorkshire are to
England, that Galilee was to Palestine. To the
Judaism of the South it was the Court of the
Gentiles; and the people, though brave and strongly
national, were charged by the Jews of the South
with errors in grammar and especially a mispro-
nunciation, which betrayed their provincialism. Here,
however, in the centre of the commercial activities
of the day, He, Who had been from all eternity
with the Father, "spake as a child," "thought as a
child," and "understood as a child,"* but, unlike
other children, as one over Whom evil had no power,
and Who never forfeited His perfect innocence.

But the word used by St. Luke implies that
the Holy Child made progress gradually and by the
use of means.† First there would be the influence
of the Virgin Mother. All that Hannah did for
Samuel, and Lois and Eunice did for Timothy, that,
and infinitely more than that, she, to whom the
Church owes the possession of the *Magnificat*, did
for the Holy Child. Then there would be the influence of the domestic rites of the weekly Sabbath and
the festal seasons of the Jewish year, all calculated

---

* I Cor. xiii. 11. In the Nazareth home, it is to be remembered, there
were also the half-brothers of the Lord, sons of Joseph by a former
marriage, James and Joses and Simon and Judas (Matt. xiii. 55),
and His sisters, whose names are not recorded.

† "With Him, as with others, wisdom widened with the years and came
into His human soul through the same channels and by the same
processes as into the souls of others." Plumptre on Luke ii. 52.

to make a deep impression on the mind at the most receptive period of human life. Then, as every town of any size had its synagogue, and every synagogue had its school, we may with reverence conceive of our Lord as receiving religious instruction from the authorized teachers, and learning in the Books of Leviticus and Deuteronomy* His earliest lessons respecting those sacrificial ordinances, which He was destined to fulfil. At Nazareth too, in conformity with the customs of His people, He was not only an obedient Son to His earthly mother, but a helper of His reputed father in his daily work or his daily trade as a carpenter, so that at a later period, it could be asked respecting Him, " Is not this the carpenter?" for the Jewish Law required that every boy should learn a trade.

How long it was before the consciousness of His high commission came upon Him we are not told.† But even when it did come, He was content " to wait for His hour." And this He did, though as day followed day and year followed year, the evils He had come into the world to redress were unceasingly working out their terrible results, provoking

---

* " The words of all the three answers to the Tempter come from two Chapters of Deuteronomy, one of which (Deut. vi.) supplied one of the passages (vi. 4-9) for the phylacteries or frontlets worn by devout Jews. The fact is every way suggestive. A prominence was thus given to that portion of the Book, which made it an essential part of the education of every Israelite. The words which our Lord used at the Temptation had, we must believe, been familiar to Him from His childhood, and He had read their meaning rightly." Plumptre on Matt. iv. 4.

† " At the age of twelve (A.D. 8) there was the first manifest unfolding of the higher life (Luke ii. 49), but, so far as we know, it stood absolutely alone, and the growth was quiet and orderly as before." Plumptre, *Excursus* on Matt. ii.

His indignation and crying for His interference. Close at hand in the Courts of Galilean tetrarchs* He would witness spectacles of baseness, disorder, and misrule, of tyranny and oppression, which must have filled His soul with holy anger. Every instance of injustice and cruelty must have excited His wrath and indignation, and seemed to cry out for His active protest and deserved reproof. But He never listened to the voices, which would prematurely have drawn Him aside from His appointed path. The "Everlasting Word" waited, fulfilling Himself His own saying afterwards, Ἐν τῇ ὑπομονῇ ὑμῶν κτήσεσθε τὰς ψυχὰς ὑμῶν,† "In your patience, or by your endurance, ye shall possess your souls." Many an impatient spirit in that region of Northern Galilee flung itself with the courage of despair against the terrible Roman legions, and in the certainty of defeat "rushed to battle, fought, and died," unable to wait as He did in preparation for His appointed hour, condensing His energies by repression and using them to sternest self-control.

The lessons, which mark the long and steadfast preparation of the Son of God for His Ministry, it is impossible to overlook. Our age is one of stimulus and high pressure. With us effect is everything. Results must be produced at once. Something to know, something to tell :—this is what men

---

* During the years spent at Nazareth Archelaus ruled with fearful cruelty as Ethnarch of Judæa ; Judas of Gamala revolted against the Roman Taxation, and gathered most of his adherents from the province of Galilee ; and Herod the Tetrarch divorced his first wife, the daughter of Aretas, and contracted an incestuous and adulterous marriage with Herodias, the daughter of his brother Aristobulus.

† Luke xxi. 19.

most eagerly desire. Few can brook obscurity or
endure to wait. Sentiment is preferred to reason,
feeling to practice, the superficial to the real, spas-
modic excitement to downright hard work. Even
in the preparation for Holy Orders there is a tendency
to shrink from waiting, and an intolerance of patient
preparation. It is too often imagined that a very
small modicum of knowledge will suffice for the discharge of the most responsible of human duties. A
greater contrast can hardly be conceived than the
modern brief,* and too often hurried, preparation
for the office of the priesthood, and the long and
quiet thirty years of preparation, which the Eternal
Word spent at Nazareth, waiting till His appointed
hour came and the Spirit bade Him go southward
towards the Jordan and commence His work. The
fact that He, the Eternal Word, persevered in His
long preparation, that He finished a perfect "home
life" before He entered on His public life, this,
when made the subject of careful meditation, cannot
fail to carry with it a divine lesson and a divine
warning against the idea that premature enthusiasm,
neglect of home duties, impatience of every day
environment, constitute in any sense a becoming
prelude to entry on the Ministerial Office.

* "The man knoweth but little of the dignity and importance of the
    priesthood, that can content himself with ordinary attainments for
    the discharge of so great and so sacred a trust; and yet he will find
    himself very much deceived, if he dependeth on the greatest per-
    fection of human knowledge without constant and fervent prayer
    to God for His grace to enable him to make a good use of it."
    R. Nelson's *Life of Bishop Bull.*

CHAPTER III.

Our Lord's abiding sense of His Divine Mission.

That the idea of a sense of Mission in its highest form pervaded our Lord's Ministry as an animating and inspiring power will be apparent to anyone on a little careful examination. Two words are employed by the Evangelists to express His sense that He had been truly *sent* by the Father to carry out His work on earth. The one, πέμπειν, simply sets forth in a general way* the relation between the sender and the sent. The other, ἀποστέλλω, the root of our word 'apostle,' brings out more strongly the representative character of an envoy;† but both are employed to describe the Mission of our Lord and His abiding sense of it, as expressed on very many occasions.

---

* See Bishop Westcott on John iv. 34. The word πέμπειν, when used of the Mission of Christ, always occurs in the aorist participle, John iv. 34; v. 23, 24, 30, 37; vi. 38, 39, 40, 44; vii. 16, 18, 28, 33.

† For ἀποστέλλω see John iii. 17, 34; v. 36; vi. 29, 57; vii. 29; viii. 42; x. 36; xi. 42; xvii. 3, 8, 18, &c.

Thus, to select a few instances out of many, during His first visit to Jerusalem after the commencement of His public Ministry, when He has told the wondering Nicodemus that the lifting up of the serpent in the wilderness was a figure of the lifting up of the Son of Man, He proceeds to inform him further that "God *sent* not the Son into the world to judge the world; but that the world should be saved through Him."*

Again, when He has been conversing with the woman of Samaria at the well of Sychar, and the returning disciples pray Him that He would eat, they are told that He has meat to eat they know not of: they ask in wonder whether any man had brought Him aught to eat, but He replies, "My meat is to do the will of Him that *sent* Me, and to accomplish His work."†

Or accompany Him into the regions of Tyre and Sidon. When the Syrophœnician woman prefers her petition on behalf of her demon-tormented daughter, and the Apostles plead that she may be sent away with her request granted, how does He answer them? "I was not *sent*," He says, "but unto the lost sheep of the house of Israel."‡

When again He is standing by the grave of Lazarus, and before He commands the stone to be rolled away He lifts up His eyes to heaven, in what words does He address the Eternal Father?

---

* John iii. 17.

† John iv. 34: see also John vi. 38, 39. "Nondum erat in medio actionis tempore Jesus, et tamen jam cogitat finem." Bengel.

‡ Matt. xv. 24.

"I thank Thee that Thou heardest Me. And I knew that Thou hearest me always: but because of the multitude which standeth around I said it, that they may believe that Thou didst *send* Me."*

Once more, when in His last high-priestly prayer He looks back upon His completed work, how striking it is that no less than six times† the sense of His Divine Mission recurs, and almost His last words before He goes forth to Gethsemane are, "O righteous Father, the world knew Thee not, but I knew Thee; and these knew that Thou didst *send* Me; and I made known unto them Thy Name."‡

Nor does the consciousness of Mission fade away after the Resurrection. When on the first Easter Day He revisits the Apostles in the upper room, He utters words of largest encouragement and assurance, saying, "As the Father hath *sent* Me, even so *send* I you." He says not, "As the Father sent Me"—as of a thing in the past, but "As the Father hath sent Me"—as a thing of the present. His Mission still goes on. The Apostles are to carry out *His* commission. They are to

---

* John xi. 41, 42, ἵνα πιστεύσωσιν ὅτι σύ (Thou and no other,) με ἀπέστειλας.

† John xvii. 3, 8, 18, 21, 23, 25.

‡ John xvii. 25, 26. Moreover the remembrance of His Mission blends itself not only with the greater, but with the less important incidents in His Ministry. When He stands up to read in the Synagogue at Nazareth (Luke iv. 18), when to teach His Apostles humility He holds the little child in His arms (Mark ix. 37), when He has received the message announcing the coming of the enquiring Greeks (John xii. 24), when He converses with the Twelve after the Institution of the Holy Eucharist (John xiv. 24), always and everywhere the thought of His Mission accompanies Him.

receive no new one.* He is Ὁ Ἀπόστολος.† They
are ἀπόστολοι. "They are in Him sharing the fulness of His power. He is in them sharing the
burden of their labours."

That the Apostles were filled with a sense of
being entrusted with a divine commission is illustrated alike in the Acts and the Epistles. The
firmness, the resolution, the defiance of danger, the
conviction that they were speaking in the name
and the power of the Republic, which entrusted
them with their commission, imbued her ambassadors
with courage to deliver her demands to barbarous
peoples; and such a feeling seems to have transfused
itself into the Apostles. The conviction that they were
entrusted with a commission from a risen and ascended
Lord carried them out of and beyond themselves.‡
The aspect, which the Christians of the Apostolic and
sub-Apostolic Ages, of the age of the Martyrs, of that
of the early Missionaries to barbarian races, presented to the world, was such as Society had never
witnessed before. It was startled, as it had never
been startled before, by the spectacle of a new order
of men linked together in an occupation as definite
as a soldier's, "for carrying on a perpetual aggression
against human ignorance and human sin, venturing

---

* Καθὼς ἀπέσταλκέ με ὁ πατήρ, κἀγὼ πέμπω ὑμᾶς. John xx. 21.
† See Bishop Westcott's *Revelation of the Risen Lord*, p. 85.
Heb. iii. 1.

‡ "It is a known fact of human character," remarks Professor Mozley,
"that a man is never so vigorous, so decided, so unchangeably
resolute and determined, so inaccessible to every attempt to divert
him from his purpose, and so elevated above every obstacle and
barrier in his way......as when he declares that he himself does
nothing and wills nothing, but is only following an unseen motion
from without." *Lectures and other Theological Papers.*

rightly on the task of teaching, comforting, warning,
elevating human souls," and proclaiming the glad
tidings of One, Who as God Incarnate had lived
man's life, and died man's death, and given that
life and that death for the Redemption of the
creatures He had made.

Such was our Lord's sense of Mission. It
is well in dealing with the Pastoral Office to go
up to Him Who was the true "Pastor Pastorum,"
and see how the sense of a great commission was
to Him a source of strength and inspiring power.
True it is that the Pastoral Office has long since
ceased to be a new thing. True it is that since the
day of Pentecost it has taken a prominent shape and
received a definite organization. Eighteen centuries
have passed over what in its idea was and is the
divinest of human employments. If it is too often
identified merely with a line of life which has its
routine, its drudgery, its mixed and imperfect
motives, its low aims and worldly maxims, this is
no more than what the history of the Jewish Church
would have led us to expect.

But there is no reason, because what was
"clear in the spring" has become "miry in the
stream," that we should fasten our eyes only on the
turbid waters instead of ascending higher to the
clear flowing fountain head. It was said by no
monastic recluse of the Middle Ages, by no modern
sacerdotalist, but by Daniel Wilson, Bishop of
Calcutta, that "a right conception of the unparalleled importance of the Christian Ministry as appointed
by Christ Himself to be the instrument of grace,

the ambassador of reconciliation, as representing
and standing in the place of the Saviour, as the
depository and pillar of the truth, as the Messenger
of the Lord of Hosts, as the Steward of the mysteries
of God, the watchman, the leader of the army, and
the Shepherd of the flock of Christ, is essential to
any great revival of religion ;" and, he adds, " there
is no surer proof of spiritual decay than a low esteem
of the sacred functions of the Pastoral Office."*

Those words, coming from whom they come,
are well deserving of attention. Belief in the reality
of the commission, which accompanies the convey-
ance of the grace of Holy Orders, has an important
bearing on the Ministerial life.† For it can *humble*,
it can *sustain*, it can *quicken*, it can *console*.

It can humble. Some seem to be afraid that
a true sense of the dignity of the Ministerial Office,
as coming through human hands from Christ Himself, tends to foster pride and arrogance. If it does,
it will be not because of, but in spite of the right
conception of its solemnity. It is not the authority
entrusted to him that the devout deacon or priest
will most appreciate in a commission coming to
him from the Head of the Church, but the solemn
responsibility of a charge so committed and so in-
curred. St. Chrysostom tells us that when he read
the words, " Obey them that have the rule over
you, and submit to them : for they watch in behalf

---

* See Bishop Wilson's Introduction to Baxter's *Reformed Pastor.*

† St. Paul speaks of himself as the chief of sinners, and yet surpasses
all other writers of the New Testament in the vigour with which
he magnifies the office which he has received from Christ.

of your souls, as they that shall give account,"* "they did cause a kind of earthquake within him, and produce a holy fear and trembling in his soul."† This can excite no surprise. For considering what the Ministry involves, who would dare to enter it, were it not that He, Who lays upon one the burden, will Himself prove the helper of the Ministry ; and He, who conferreth the dignity, will give the strength to uphold one in it ? He who stands in Canterbury Cathedral ‡ and surveys the tomb of Archbishop Chichele, where the living man in all his pomp is contrasted with the bare skeleton beneath him, is reminded in the most forcible manner of the awful difference between the pompous trappings of any outward dignity,§ and the spectacle that the most exalted will present, when he

* Heb. xiii. 17.

† Bishop Bull's *Sermons ; Works*, vol. i., p. 160.

‡ See Stanley's *Memorials of Canterbury*, p. 157.

§ "Is self-importance the natural result of belief in the reality of the Ministerial call and commission ? Is it certain that a clergy, which should profess to have no authority or power whatever beyond their lay brethren, and shall nevertheless undertake to teach and feed Christ's people solely on the ground of individual merit, would be more entirely free from self-importance than are the clergy of the Church ? Is not that which is personal, individual, proper to a man himself, more likely to minister to this sense of self-importance, than that which he enjoys only in common with every member of a vast corporation, and which implies nothing that distinguishes him among or above his clerical brethren ? " Liddon, p. 27. When St. Bernard congratulates Pope Eugenius III. on his new position, he does not merely write to him as a privileged friend, but he addresses him in a strain persons occupying such a position seldom listen to. He bids him strip from his eyes all veils and disguises, and reminds him that, exalted as is his position, it involves not pre-eminence in dignity, but pre-eminence in labour. He exhorts him to forget the robes he wears, the gems which sparkle in his tiara, the precious metals which adorn his palace, his vast influence over the Western World, and to regard them as no more enduring than morning mists, which will soon have passed away for ever. St. Bernard's *De Consideratione*, ii. 8, 18.

is removed by the hand of death. No one can find in a call to the Ministry anything that can really excite feelings of pride and self-exaltation. He cannot but be far more likely to enter into the words of St. Francis of Assisi, "A man is as great as he is in the sight of God, and no greater." He who has learnt, in however imperfect a degree, to appreciate the force of St. Paul's words, "I live, (and) yet not I, but Christ liveth in Me," and understands what a call to work for Christ means, will show that a true sense of Mission from Christ is compatible with the most genuine humility. "From my earliest childhood," said one on the day of his ordination, "it has been my deepest wish to enter Holy Orders. God has fulfilled my wish for me. He can give me no more. Let me dedicate myself to Him." No one had a keener sense of Mission. But no one had more of the grace of modesty.

But while the sense of Mission humbles, it also *sustains*. When the day of Ordination is over with its inevitable strain and excitement, and the newly-ordained deacon or priest has settled down to the routine of every day life, then he begins to feel the strength or the weakness of his moral and spiritual fibre. A man cannot fail to find himself confronted from time to time with circumstances, which will call out all the reality and all the courage he possesses, and force him to set his face as a flint, and "speak boldly as he ought to speak." Then he will feel as Moses felt, when he said unto God, "Oh Lord, I am not eloquent, neither heretofore, nor since Thou hast spoken unto Thy servant;"* or as Gideon, when he said, "Oh Lord, wherewith shall I save Israel? my family is the poorest in Manasseh."† What was the answer to the former? "I AM hath *sent* thee....I will be with thy mouth."‡ What was the answer to the latter? "Surely I will be with thee." § Here was the source of encouragement flowing from a sense of Mission, and this sense of Mission has helped to win many victories in the history of the Church. It armed an Ambrose with a boldness exceeding that of any Roman ambassador, and enabled him to forbid the entry into his church of a Theodosius, stained as he was with the blood of the people of Thessalonica. It enabled Anselm to stand firm and unmoved before the fiercest opposition of a worldly age. It strengthened him to speak with power and to secure at the same time the respect of the most licentious of English kings. What they did on a great scale, if we remember we have a commission from on high, we can do on a smaller yet not a less important scale. The very same I AM, who encouraged Moses, Joshua, Gideon, and the Saints of old, now sits in majesty at the right hand of God. He calls us by incidents of our own lives, which carry with them their own evidence, and which we cannot believe to be accidental, by guidings which we cannot fail to recognise, to devote our lives to His service. He claims us for His own, and He will impart the strength we need. What are we that we should be ambassadors for Christ? "Simply nothing, save so far as He is

* Exod. iv. 10.   † Judges vi. 15.   ‡ Exod. iv. 12.
                     § Judges vi. 16.

pleased to use us," but everything through Him,
Who by the voice of His servant in the Ordination
Service* saith to us :—

"Take thou authority to execute the office of
a Deacon in the Church of God, committed unto thee ;

"Receive the Holy Ghost for the office and
work of a Priest in the Church of God, now committed unto thee by the imposition of our hands."

But a sense of Mission can not only sustain,
it can also *quicken.* It does not, alas ! require the
experience of many years in Holy Orders to know
that the oil of early zeal and fervour can dwindle
in the lamp of the soul. St. Paul did not deem his
own son Timothy incapable of yielding to the most
subtle, though most common temptation to become
slack and remiss, to become ready to acquiesce with
fatal ease in very average standards of devotion.
He exhorts him, with all the earnestness of one who
knew his time was short, to "stir up," to "fan
afresh into a flame"† the gift that was in him by
the imposition of Apostolic hands. The Vestal
Virgin at Rome could not be more solemnly warned
to tend the eternal flame on the public hearth‡ than
is the Bishop of the Church of Ephesus reminded
by the Apostle of nurturing and tending the grace of
ordination which he had received. And if Timothy
needed the warning, much more do we; and that, from
the very fact that in clerical life religion is a man's
profession and employment. No one in Holy Orders

---

* Bishop Westcott's *Thoughts from the Ordinal,* p. 28.

† Ἀναζωπυρεῖν, II Timothy i. 6 : sopitos ignes suscitare.

‡ "Custodiant ignem foci publici sempiternum." *Cicero de Legibus,* xi. 8.

has failed to recognise the truth of Bishop Butler's remarks on the serious effect of the repetition of passive impressions.† "It requires double diligence," observes Richard Cecil in his valuable remarks on the Clerical Character, "to avoid going through the acts of religion mechanically, and to maintain the spirit of religion while performing the acts of religion"...."I have prayed," he writes, "I have talked, I have preached; but now I shall perish after all, if I do not feed on the bread I have broken to others."‡

But a sense of Mission can also *console*.

It may seem ungracious at the commencement or in the immediate prospect of ministerial work to whisper even the necessity for consolation. But it is wisest to look facts steadily in the face. Failure and disappointment are to a certain extent inevitable in well-nigh every Ministry. We set out with our ideals. We form our magnificent plans. We do not see the obstacles in our way. We do not anticipate discomfiture. We forget that disappointment has been meted out in a large measure to many master-builders in the Church of God :—to Moses, who led his people out of Egypt, to die himself in view of the Land of Promise, which he was never to enter :—to Samuel, who guided his country safely through the shock of change, only to witness the degeneracy of his own sons, and the sad sunset of Saul's career :—to Isaiah, who strengthened

† Butler's *Analogy*, pt. i., ch. v. See also Paley's Sermon before the University of Cambridge, 1794.

‡ *Cecil's Remains*, iv., p. 522.

the good Hezekiah to resist the Assyrian invader, but himself suffered at the hands of his son Manasseh : —to John the Baptist, of whom our Lord Himself affirmed that a greater "had never been born of woman," but who at the very outset of his wonderful career fell by the sword of a Galilean tetrarch. "In the distance," it has been said,* "such failure has a splendour of its own. Ages of veneration have traced round it a nimbus, which diverts attention from the historic reality. But at the time it was very hard to bear. Disappointment brings temptations to impatient words and impatient actions, or, worse still, to suppressed gloom, which issues in chronic discontent with work or with life, or even in the gradual growth of an indifference to truth and duty." This, or somewhat like it, happens oftener than is suspected; and the degree, in which a man can resist the temptations which disappointment entails, depends very much on the complexion of his inner life in earlier years, and the sincerity and single-heartedness with which he has devoted himself to the work of the Ministry.

If, however, the desire to take Holy Orders has been a subject of anxious scrutiny ; if it has been accompanied with sincere prayer for guidance ; if with the advice of friends there has been a real effort to ascertain the will of God respecting us ; then having a good conscience we can leave results to Him, and fall back on the sense of our commission. He Who assigns the charge with its conditions, its environments, its responsibilities, and its inevitable

* Canon Liddon, *The Moral Value of a Mission from Christ,* p. 24.

trials, He alone can rightly estimate the account to which we have turned it.* Even to the last we are poor and incompetent judges of what constitutes true success. Never did more complete discomfiture seem to have crowned any enterprise† than when Pilate uttered the irrevocable word, "Let Him be crucified." Thirty years of secluded preparation at Nazareth, three years of mingled acceptance and rejection during His actual Ministry, the flight of His disciples, the bitterness of the Cross, seemed to proclaim that nothing had been achieved. But looking back upon those years the Chief Shepherd, whose motto had been, "My meat is to do the will of Him that *sent* Me, and to accomplish His work," could exclaim in the note of a conqueror, "It is finished." And if this was so with Him, shall not those, whom He calls to be His Ministers and to follow in His steps, resolve to think less of outward success and more of faithfulness to their divine commission?

* Bishop Westcott, *Thoughts from the Ordinal*, p. 54.

† "Spernere mundum, spernere neminem, spernere seipsum, spernere sperni,"—St. Bernard's motto.

CHAPTER IV.

OUR LORD'S LIFE OF PRAYER IN THE MIDST OF UNWEARIED ACTIVITY.

From our Lord's abiding sense of His Divine Mission we pass on to consider His Life of Prayer in the midst of unwearied activity.

A suitable introduction will be supplied by an incident recorded in the first Chapter of St. Mark's Gospel. It is connected with the first Sabbath that He is recorded to have spent at Capernaum. Early in the morning He repairs to the Synagogue, and after astonishing those present by the authority with which He taught,* delivers a miserable demoniac from the power that enthralled him,† and then, probably about mid-day, retires with four of His disciples to the home of St. Peter, and heals his mother-in-law of a violent fever.‡ Then, when the sun has set, He ministers to the stream of sick and impotent folk, whom the news of the miracle has attracted to the Apostle's house, and heals many.§ What follows when night closes in

---

* Mark i. 22. † Mark i. 27. ‡ Mark i. 30. § Luke iv. 40.

on that Sabbath of holy activities? "Very early,
while it was yet dark,"* we read that He "arose"
and made His way towards a lonely spot near the
town, and there was engaged in prayer, till He
was interrupted by the coming of the Apostles
headed by St. Peter to announce that "all men
were seeking Him."†

Here we have a rift in the outward history
of our Lord, and are permitted to catch a glimpse
behind the veil of His inner Life. We are permitted
to take note how the occupations of the busiest
Ministry, so busy that we scarcely ever read of
His meals or His rest, were combined with constant
communion by prayer with Him, of Whom He
could say, "I and My Father are one."

We find Prayer ushering in all the important epochs of His Ministry. By Prayer at the
moment of His Baptism He consecrates Himself to
the great task of His earthly Life.‡ By a whole
night of Prayer He prepares for the solemn choice
of His Apostles.§ By Prayer He prepares for the
Transfiguration, and is actually thus engaged, when
His Body becomes radiant with celestial light.¶
By His solemn high-priestly Prayer in the upper
room He consecrates Himself on the eve of His
Passion for the supreme act of self-renunciation.‖
By thrice repeated supplications He defeats the
final temptation of the evil one in Gethsemane.** In

---

* Mark i. 35, πρωῒ ἔννυχα λίαν.   † Mark i. 37, πάντες ζητοῦσί σε.
‡ Luke iii. 21.   § Luke vi. 12.   ¶ Luke ix. 28, 29.   ‖ John xvii. 1—26.
** Matt. xxvi. 36; Luke xxii. 40—44.

words of Prayer He intercedes for His murderers
as He is nailed to His Cross.*

From time to time also we notice how in
the very thick of His work He *made* opportunities
for retirement and prayer. On one occasion we
find Him avoiding the multitude that thronged
Him, and withdrawing into the deserts that He
might engage in Prayer.† On another we are told
how His disciples watched Him while thus engaged
and asked Him to "teach them to pray, as John
also taught his disciples."‡ Again, after feeding the
five thousand, when the multitudes wish to take
Him and make Him a King, He retires to the
mountain-range to pray before He reveals Himself
to the tempest-tost Apostles by walking on the Lake.§
These incidents will suffice to indicate what lay
behind His incarnate Life, so " complete, so balanced,
so harmonious, in working out its course without
violence or strain," "never idle, but never busy, ever
at work, but never hurried, like the daily and
yearly march of nature, at once so mighty, so
equable, and so still."¶ There lay behind the outer
life the inner life of prayer, meditation, and communion with His Father in heaven. He was not
satisfied merely with a constant direction of His
soul in Prayer, but He has special times and seasons
for Prayer and retirement, and so while He does
what is most human, He makes us ever feel He is
living absolutely in the Divine.

---

* Luke xxiii. 34.
† Luke v. 15, 16, ἦν ὑποχωρῶν ἐν ταῖς ἐρήμοις καὶ προσευχόμενος.
‡ Luke xi. 1—3.   § John vi. 15.   ¶ Dean Church's *Sermons*, p. 172.

Moreover He not only resorts to Prayer Himself, but inculcates it on others. Not only does
He give His Apostles a distinct Form of Prayer,
but He bids them "ask," and assures them that
they shall "receive," "knock, and it shall be opened
unto them"; and to encourage even importunity in
Prayer He delivers the Parables of the Friend
at Mid-night,* and of the Widow and the Unjust
Judge,† while he specially commends the faith of
the lonely Syrophœnician woman, who persevered
in her petition in spite of silence, refusal, and reproach.‡ Thus it is plain that He regarded Prayer
not merely as a dreamy reverie, or the half-passive
play of sentiment or emotional ecstacy, but as a
distinct and solemn work, "the one department of
action in which man realizes the highest privilege and
capacity of his being."§ Those who are inclined to
deem Prayer "less worthy of the energies of a
thinking man than hard work," and whisper that
it is an excellent thing for a recluse or a senti-
mentalist, for women and children, have plainly
much to learn from the Ministry of Him, Who
was at once perfect God and perfect Man.

Thus the "Pastor Pastorum" prayed earnestly
and systematically; and therefore those, who are
called to feed His sheep, and dispense His Word
and Sacraments, cannot deny that herein especially they must "endeavour themselves" to
follow His example. Now one of the exhortations
of the Bishop to candidates for ordination is that

* Luke xi. 8.   † Luke xviii. 1—8.   ‡ Matthew xv. 21.
§ Liddon's *Elements of Religion*, p. 170.

they will pray earnestly for "God's Holy Spirit," and one of the promises they make is that, "the Lord being their helper," they will be "diligent in Prayer" both public and private. And of this a man may be assured, that, however many may be the distractions incident to ministerial work, however little time* he may have to call his own, if he is to rise above the dead level of an easy-going professionalism, if he is to be a man of collectedness and self-control, there is one thing he must secure, and that is time to be "alone with himself, alone with God, and those eternal realities which are behind the rush and confusion of mortal things." If in the Pastoral Office he would really help the souls of others, he must have learnt himself in some measure that practically there are but two things in the Universe, his soul and the God Who made it, that "he has a depth within him, an infinite abyss of existence, and the scene in which he bears part for a moment is but a gleam of sunshine upon its surface."†

It is recorded of Robertson of Brighton that when in the autumn of 1846 he sought the solitude and silence of the Tyrol, his soul, left to explore its own recesses and to feel its nothingness in the presence of Infinitude,‡ laid its foundations deep and sure ; and he emerged from the clouds which had settled down upon him into a radiance,

---

* " If we understand in any measure what our faith is, we cannot ever think that the busiest occupation can dispense with silent, solemn meditation on the mysteries which we are commissioned to dispense." Bishop Westcott, *Thoughts from the Ordinal*, p. 74.

† Newman's *Sermons*, vol. i., p. 23 ; *Apologia*, p. 59.

‡ See the Life of Robertson.

which, though it did not always abide with him in
its full clearness, yet never again wholly left him;
and henceforth, "unhasting yet unresting," he gave
himself up to make full proof of his Ministry.* It is
indeed a false religion to say that a man's own
soul needs his *exclusive* care, but it is more false to
say that amidst the activities and industries of life
it needs none. We may depend upon it that the
outward disclosure of a noble character,† the great
unexpected deed, done, as it were, by a momentary
flash of heroic force, comes not without preparation.
Deeds of self-sacrifice and self-renunciation "tell
of long and secret converse with high thoughts and
resolutions, and with Him Who gives and inspires
them."‡

Now as regards the cultivation of the devotional habit, the want of which Richard Cecil
used to say was "the leading defect in Christian
Ministers." It is undeniable that those who give
most time to prayer, "give but little, when it is
meted out in the measure of antiquity." Still it is
to be remembered that we live in an age and a
country in which the energies of those, who seriously
labour for the cause and kingdom of Christ, are
taxed to an unparalleled extent; and there is great
danger lest the business, the strain, and the distrac-
tion of daily life should wear down and deaden the

* Principal Tulloch's *Movements of Religious Thought*, pp. 306, 307.
† "The habit I recommend as the foundation of almost all the great ones,
   is *retirement*. Were I required to comprise my advice to a young
   clergyman in one sentence it should be this, *Learn to live alone*. Half
   of your faults arise from the want of this faculty." Paley's *Advice
   to the younger Clergy of the Diocese of Carlisle*, p. 71.
   ‡ Dean Church's *Human Life and its Conditions*, p. 59.

habit of devotion. We must therefore be on our
guard against any temptation to neglect the claims
of "the interior life." "The hardest and greatest
preparation," writes good George Herbert,* "lies
within." To maintain devotion in daily life is no
easy matter. "Hic labor, hoc opus est." And here
we must settle it with ourselves that devotion, like
every other religious habit, must be disciplined.†
Just as in the practical matters of life it will never
do to live without plan and simply trusting to
unregulated habits of duty, so it will not do as
regards Prayer.

No one ever lived a more busy life than the
late Bishop Wilberforce. The amount of work
of the most varied kinds which he got through,
astonishes us when we peruse his Life. But what
do we find him laying down in his Diary on his
appointment to the Episcopate? "I propose mark-
ing down here," he writes, "a few practical rules,
as they occur to me for my guidance. May God
help me to keep them for Christ's sake! The first
great necessity seems to be to maintain a devotional
temper. The first great peril is secularity. I would
remember that it must be guarded against by
living in prayer, and ever keeping in mind that,

> 'To serve God
> In His way
> Through His Grace
> Is all.'

* Compare the words of S. T. Coleridge when he heard those about him
speaking of prayer. "Prayer," he said, "Prayer! It is so hard to
pray," and then he burst into a flood of tears.

† Bishop Westcott's *Disciplined Life*, p. 4.

" Trusting, therefore, in God's help, without which
I well know by my own experience that all attempts
at spending time devotionally are utterly vain, I
resolve—

' 1st Resolution :

'As my universal Rule, when not hindered by
illness, or some impossibility, to secure at least one
hour before breakfast for devotional exercises.'

Next, as my great fear is that of acting with
an eye to men and myself rather than God, I
resolve—

' 2nd Resolution :

' Often to set my conduct and principles in
the light of the coming day, and try thus to form
the habit of acting under the eye of God.' "*

These Rules are well worthy of being remembered, for we cannot have to live busier lives than
he who drew them up. Like the great Bishop we
can resolve to bring our devotions under discipline,
and not allow them to become sporadic, random,
hap-hazard efforts. By a habit of early rising,
which will by effort become a second nature, we
can give to God the freshness of the morning's
thoughts, and see that the early prayers of the
morning have precedence of everything else. And
if besides we strive, by putting up short ejaculatory
prayers† from time to time, to cultivate what
Keble calls " an earnest practice of the Presence

---

* *Life of Bishop Wilberforce*, vol. i., p. 319.
† The late Bishop of Brechin dwells on the value of " ejaculatory prayer,
especially such as is full of confidence and love." Bishop of Brechin,
p. 35.

of God," we shall be enabled to maintain a devotional spirit in the midst of the most distracting engagements, which will enable us instead of brooding over the imperfections of our daily work, to present it with all its blemishes as a sacrifice to Christ. " Thou, God, seest me " may be a brief sentence to remember, but how many difficulties would be smoothed, how many temptations would be overcome, how many things would be lightened, if from time to time during the day it was thoughtfully and earnestly repeated !

But if the devotional spirit ought to be applied to anything,* it is to the study of the Holy Scriptures. " Scripture is a devotional book essentially, and it appeals to a devotional spirit."† The critical study of the Bible is one thing, the devotional study is quite another. The latter mode of study is within the reach of the simple, but it ought on no account to be neglected by the scholar, though his intellectual habits are very apt to tempt him to pass it by. When Thomas à Kempis is treating of the studies of " the Brothers of the Common Life," he bids the brethren before commencing their study of Scripture to say always, " Speak, Lord, for Thy servant heareth ;" and he assures them that He, Whose word it is, " will speak to their souls and hold converse with them." And this is the true spirit in which our Ordinal

---

* Henry Martyn tells us how much amidst the tumult of an examination in the Senate House he owed to the steadying thought of God, and a single prayer for self-recollectedness. The agitation and excitement quickly passed away and there was a great calm.

† Bishop Woodford's *Great Commission*, p. 49.

would have us approach the Word of God, which
it sets before us with solemn emphasis as "the
central object of our personal study, the treasury
of our public teaching, the final standard of all
necessary doctrine."* He who imagines that the
necessity for the careful study of the Scriptures is
over when Holy Orders have been obtained, or that
he "fairly knows" his Bible, shows that he has
not adequately measured his Ordination vow, and
gives but little ground of hope as regards his
spiritual progress either for himself or his people.
It is then that the necessity for a more deeply
devotional study begins. Then the revelations of
Scripture are no longer matters to be pondered in the
closet, but to be applied, like a refiner's fire, to
his own heart and the hearts of others. Then if he
goes to the Scriptures with all the general and
special knowledge he has acquired, and at the same
time with that humble and teachable spirit which
Thomas à Kempis so much insisted on, he will
catch, now in this incident, now in that, a vision
of the Divine Worker; and, assured that as He
wrought in old times so He works still, he will
hear the voice of a Person speaking behind the
Book to his own soul; and catching its meaning,
he will bring it forth as an instructed scribe for
the comfort and encouragement of his people.†

Towards such a study of Holy Scripture Meditation is a great help. Meditation has been defined
by an old author to be "rei cujusvis in mente

---

* Bishop Westcott's *Thoughts from the Ordinal*, p. 19.
† See the Bishop of Ely's *Great Commission*, p. 50.

repetitio et agitatio quædam." Archbishop Benson
defined it as "the exercise of all the powers of the
soul in the apprehension of God;" and Principal
Shairp in his "Religion and Culture" speaks of it
as "the quiet, serious, devout fixing of the mind
on some great truth or fact of religion, holding it
before the mind steadily, silently brooding over it,
till it becomes warm and vital and melts into us."*
Calling into play as it does the imagination, understanding, affection, and will, it tends to render the
devotional study of the Word really profitable; and
a man, who steadily practises it, will find the truths
of the Bible becoming more and more living realities;
and instead of gathering up views and opinions
learnt second-hand, he will find himself guided to
what is far better than theological conclusions, and
that is theological convictions, and will become
riper and fuller in knowledge of the Scriptures, and
of Him Who speaks through them to the soul.
"Suffer me earnestly to intreat you," wrote the
Missionary Brainerd to a candidate for Missionary
work, "to give yourself to prayer, to reading, and
to *meditation on divine truths.*" Richard Baxter
in his "Saint's Everlasting Rest" observes that
our speaking to ourselves in Meditation should go
before our speaking to God in Prayer. For want of
attending to the due order, men speak to God with
less reverence and affection than they would speak
to an angel, if he should appear to them, or to a
judge, if they were speaking for their lives. "*Speaking*

---

* *Religion and Culture.* "Lectio inquirit, oratio postulat, meditatio
 invenit, contemplatio disgustat." St. Augustine. See Bridges'
 Christian Ministry, p. 209.

to the God of heaven in prayer," he continues, *" is a weightier duty* than men are aware of."*

And here one suggestion may be made, and that is that it is a valuable help to a man as regards the cultivation of the devotional habit to make up by degrees his own little Manual of Devotion, copying out from various Manuals and Biographies of holy men, Prayers, Confessions, Acts of Faith, Intercessions, Thanksgivings, and adding to them from time to time. It was thus gradually that the 'Devotions of Bishop Andrewes' was built up; and his biographer writes of it, "Had you seen the original MS., happy in the glorious deformity thereof, being worn, slubbered with his pious hands, and watered with his penitential tears, you would have been forced to confess that it belonged to no other than pure and primitive Devotion."† And here it is to be borne in mind that the Prayer Book itself can supply to a remarkable extent much that is needed for such a Manual. The Collects, which, in the words of Macaulay, "have soothed the griefs of forty generations of Christians," will be found as deep and full in their application to the varied needs and trials of "mind, body, and estate," amidst this bustling twentieth century, as when they were made to give way to the "Directory of a Puritan Faction."‡ No one can attentively study the Prayer Book without being impressed by the way in which it adapts itself to the wants of "all conditions of men."

* Baxter's *Saint's Everlasting Rest*, chap. xvi.
† Bishop of Ely's *Memoir*, p. 218.
‡ Macaulay's *History of England*, i., p. 160.

C

In such a Book a prominent place ought to be
given first to *Intercession*, and secondly to *Thanksgiving*.

Intercession. One of the first Resolutions that
Bishop Wilberforce makes on his appointment to
the episcopate is,* " I will form a regular systematic
habit of intercession for my clergy ;" and when
Mr. Gladstone visited Bishop Hamilton of Salisbury
in his last illness, he found him with a map of his
diocese spread out before him, interceding by name
for the various parishes and clergy it contained.†
The privilege of Intercession was illustrated under
the Jewish Dispensation in the dress of the High
Priest. While on his shoulders he bore two onyx
stones inscribed with the names of the twelve tribes,‡
on his breast-plate he wore the same names inscribed on four rows of stones, placed there, over
his heart, the seat of the affections. In this position
they symbolized the personal interpenetration of his
life with those for whom he interceded, and whom
he represented before God. This significant figure
received its fulfilment and reality in the Person of
the One Great High Priest, "Who ever liveth to
make intercession for us." It is illustrated also in
the intercessory prayers of the great Apostle St.
Paul for the Roman, Corinthian, Ephesian Christians, and indeed for every member of the Churches
which he founded, and to which He ministered. He
Who Himself gave His divine picture-book of type
and symbol to the Jewish Law-giver, has specially

* Life, vol. i., p. 319.
† See Liddon's *Memoir of Bishop Hamilton*.   ‡ Exod. xxviii. 29.

made it part of our love to Him to intercede for
one another, as He intercedes for us.* And when
we feel cold and dry ourselves, and seem hardly able
to frame a prayer for ourselves, we can often rise
into a higher sphere altogether by laying aside all
thought for ourselves, and remembering before God
those we know to be in trial or temptation. And
he who has felt what it is to pray for others, knows
how it brings with it its own reward. " Praying for
people ahead of me," wrote General Gordon in his
diary, "whom I am about to visit, gives me much
strength." Nothing is more noticeable in Bishop
Andrewes' Devotions† than the wide sweep of his
Intercessions for

"My College, My Parish,
Southwell, St. Paul's, Westminster,
Dioceses of Chichester, Ely, and my present,
Clergy, people, helps, governments."

Thanksgiving also is ever to be combined with
Intercession. The combination of Thanksgiving and
Intercession is one of the distinguishing marks of
St. Paul's Epistles in contrast with anything which
is found in those of St. James, St. Peter or St. John.‡
And it is our duty and our privilege to give to our
prayers an eucharistic as well as an intercessory
character. If we remember always to thank God

---

* "The true dignity of the Christian Ministry consists not in the self-
sufficient isolation of incommunicable power, but in the keen sense of
nearest affinity with the great Body of the Faithful, of the interpenetration of its life with the life of the Body. To be in closest bond and
sympathy is by its very organization its highest perfection." *The
Great Commission*, p. 220.

† Bishop Andrewes' *Devotions*, p. 31.

‡ Dean Howson's *Hulsean Lectures*, p. 143.

for shaping the turnings and windings of our lives
towards our present position, if we acknowledge His
hand in advancing us to the dignity of the diaconate
or the priesthood, if we trace His voice in so often
calling and recalling us when we were going astray,
if we habitually ascribe to Him any measure of
success we may have gained, we shall enter into
the spirit of David, that great Master of Thanksgiving, when he wrote, "Bless the Lord, O my
soul, and forget not all His benefits." We shall
find ourselves cultivating more and more that spirit
of thankfulness, which Bishop Andrewes exhibits in
his Devotions, when he writes,

> "I thank Thee, O Lord, my God,
> For my being, life, reason ;
> For nurture, protection, guidance ;
> For education, civil rights, religion ;
> For Thy gifts of grace, nature, fortune ;
> For redemption, regeneration, catechizing ;
> For my call, recall, and many calls besides ;
> For thy forbearance, long-suffering,
> Long, long-suffering,
> To me-ward,
> Many seasons, many years, up to this time."

It is recorded of Dr. Arnold that about three
weeks before his death "he seemed to have felt
quite a rush of love in his heart towards God in
Christ," and he remarked that the thought of his
life so full of comforts was very startling, when
contrasted with the lot of millions whose life is so
full of distress and trouble. These eucharistic
thoughts may well be deemed preparatory to the

end that came so soon; and the Minister of Christ,
who perseveres in Intercession and Thanksgiving,
will be best preparing for the coming in the first
watch or the second watch of Him, Who during
His Incarnate Life again and again gave thanks to
His Heavenly Father, and therein set us an example
to follow.

CHAPTER V.

Our Lord's discharge of His Prophetical Office.

We now pass on to consider our Lord's example as a Preacher. It is the fourth Chapter of St. Luke's Gospel, which brings this most prominently before us. In this chapter we have an account of His rising for the first time to acknowledge His call to the prophetical office. It was in the synagogue of His native Nazareth.* The occasion was one of singular interest. The Lesson from the Law had been read. That from the Prophets was to follow. Then His rising up was a sign that He was willing to read,† and the servant of the Synagogue handed Him the scroll containing the prophecies of Isaiah. Having read the prescribed portion from the sixty-first Chapter, He paused, rolled up the scroll, returned it to the attendant, and sat down.‡

His sitting down was a sign that He was ready to give His "Midrash" or Explanation. And

* Luke iv. 16.   † Luke iv. 17.   ‡ Ἐκάθισε, Luke iv. 20.

He proceeded to affirm that the words of the prophet had that day been fulfilled in Himself. What
" the gracious words" were, in which He expressed
this, we are not told. All we know is that in the
full confidence inspired by His divine Mission, He
declared that He had been anointed to " preach
the gospel to the poor," to " proclaim release to
the captives" and "recovering of sight to the blind,"
to "set at liberty them that are bruised," and "to
proclaim the acceptable year of the Lord."* Thus
He formally accepted the call marked out for Him,
and acknowledged the claims upon Himself of the
prophetical office.

This office He not only acknowledged Himself,
but He solemnly charged it upon His Apostles,
first when He sent them forth on their earliest tenta-
tive mission,† and secondly in His last charge just
before His Ascension.‡ The importance of the
office was naturally felt by the Apostles, and we
find St. Paul dwelling on it again and again. Not
only does he claim for himself the title of a "herald,"§
who comes in the name of a king, and is therefore
for the time endowed with a king's dignity and
authority; but he dwells with solemn emphasis on
the fact that Christ sent him to preach, and he
declares, "Woe is unto me, if I preach not the gospel."‖
The Christian Priest, therefore, shares Christ's prophetical office, and it is no wonder that its functions
receive express mention in the Prayer Book and

* Luke iv. 21.   † Luke ix. 2.   ‡ Mark xvi. 15.   § I Tim. ii. 7.
‖ " Væ mihi si non evangelizavero," (I Cor. ix. 16,)—the inscription
round the great Bell of St. Paul's.

the Articles. In the Litany we pray that God will " illuminate all Bishops, Priests, and Deacons with true knowledge and understanding of His Word, that both by their *preaching* and living they may set it forth and show it accordingly." Again in the Ordination Service the Bishop says to the newly ordained Priest, " Be thou a faithful Dispenser of the Word of God........Take thou authority to preach the Word of God."* Once more in the twenty-third and twenty-sixth Articles it is laid down that no man can take upon him the office of preaching, unless he be first lawfully called and sent by those having authority so to do in Christ's Church.

Sharing, therefore, as he does, Christ's prophetical office, a Christian Minister is bound to strive after excellence in this department of his work ; for though there is sometimes a tendency to exaggerate the function of the preacher, and to place it on a level with or even above the administration of the Sacraments, yet its purport and object are undeniably of the utmost moment. For preaching may be truly defined to be the " authoritative delivery of a message from God to men for the salvation of their souls." For its adequate discharge, therefore, it demands certain moral and spiritual qualifications. Amongst these may be enumerated :—

(i) *The sense of a divine mission.*

Such a sense specially applies to the office of Preaching. Without a divine commission it is

* See the Office for the Ordering of Priests.

without any authority. Based upon such a commission, and exercised under a corresponding sense of responsibility, it carries with it the pledge of divine help and special blessing.*

(ii) *Personal holiness.*

Everything depends on the complexion of the inward life. If a man's " life is lightning, he can make his words thunder," but not otherwise. St. Paul's words on this point are decisive. Writing to Timothy, he says, *Take heed unto thyself and unto the doctrine*†—to thyself first : then to the doctrine. For " a holy sermon is but for an hour : a holy life is a perpetual sermon."‡

(iii) *Purity of intention.*

This implies purity of intention in seeking Holy Orders originally, the absence of low motives, the absence of self-consciousness ; for, as St. Chrysostom says, κενοδοξία, vanity, is the great stumbling-block of the Preacher.§

* See Bishop Woodford's *Ordination Sermons*, p. 189.

† I Tim. iv. 16.

‡ Leighton on I Peter iii. 1. " Vita clerici est evangelium populi."

§ " I will be sure to live well," said George Herbert on the day of his induction to Bemerton, " because the virtuous life of a Clergyman is the most powerful eloquence to persuade all that see it to reverence and love."

" Purity and sincerity of intention impart so much of their own blessed character to the whole conduct, that every act of the life becomes instinct with an energy and force which enable it to beat down opposition, and at the same time with a tenderness and patience which give to it a most winning persuasiveness in dealing with others."   Bishop Wilberforce, *Ordination Addresses*, p. 22.   " We should never rise from our knees in the morning until in our secret prayer we have earnestly asked God to keep through the day our intention pure." Ibid., p. 30, see p. 31.

(iv)   *The habit of prayer.*

If prayer is essential to the devotional study of
Holy Scripture, it is still more so in making it the
vehicle of instruction and exhortation to others.
He who asks God to speak to him that he may
speak with profit to others, will find the aid
solicited bestowed freely by Him, Who "giveth
liberally and upbraideth not." In this matter a
habit of prayerfulness is of inestimable importance,
for prayerfulness is more than prayer.

(v)   *Study.*

And if these qualifications are essential to the
prophetical office, its adequate discharge requires of
us careful *study*. In what does this consist? It
consists in the study (*a*) of the Word, (*b*) of books,
(*c*) of men, (*d*) of ourselves.

(1)   *Of the Word.*

This we must read:—

(*a*)   *Devotionally*, that God may speak to us
in it before we speak to others;

(*b*)   *Critically*, that we may interpret it cor-
rectly, and rightly divide the word of
truth, avoiding loose, inaccurate state-
ments and careless declarations of
doctrine, which make preachers "un-
awares the slayers of souls."*

(2)   *Of books.*

In the Ordinal the Bishop reminds us of
engaging in such studies as a help to
the knowledge of the Word of God.

* *Life of Bishop Wilberforce*, vol. iii., p. 95.

Especially we should study Scriptural
Topography and Geography, the History of the Church, Biographies of the
Saints and holy men, Poetry, and
Literature, and, if possible, some branch
of Natural Science, that in intellectual
no less than spiritual acquirements we
may become "riper and stronger" for
the service of the Master.

(3) *Of men.*

The knowledge of others is essential if
we would show men to themselves.
As Prophets and Teachers we are in-
terested in everything that is human.
And we are bound to obtain as far as
possible an insight into the character
of those we have to lead; noting the
passions which are strongest, and the
good qualities which are weakest in
them ; and remembering that nothing
which stirs, or attracts, or troubles our
people ought to be too great or too
little for us.*

(4) *Of ourselves.*

To use the words of George Herbert,
"the Parson's own heart and conscience
constitute his best Library." And of
the Ars Artium, the Art of winning
souls, it is especially true that well-
nigh everything depends on our being

---

* Bishop Woodford's *Great Commission*, p. 223; Dean Church's *Human
Life and its Conditions.*

able, out of the fulness of our own
hearts and experience, to tell our
people of what we ourselves have
known and felt as regards sin, pardon,
grace, and the blessedness of reconciliation with God.

There never was more need than now of such
study consistently and perseveringly maintained.
Never was more required of the Clergy, never was
there more need of adaptation to the new wants,
new demands, new modes of thought, new conditions of our modern times. Everywhere minds
are busy asking questions, pushing conclusions,
examining foundations, interpreting facts. Everywhere men and women are asking for some help,
some guidance, some clue to the problems of
existence ; and when they come to us who have
been called to the prophetical office, they have a
right to expect some proof, if not of knowledge on
our part, at least of genuine labours, such as
skilled workmen expect to find in specimens of
mechanical art. We must ever bear in mind St.
Paul's words, "I am debtor both to Greeks and
to Barbarians, both to the wise and to the
foolish."* Our Blessed Lord never forgot the twofold debt. His congregation that Sabbath morning
at Nazareth consisted chiefly of obscure peasants,
burly Galilean boatmen, toiling women, and a few
of the better class. But He gave them of His best,
and "they marvelled at the gracious words which
proceeded out of His mouth." What He did then

* Rom. i. 14.

He did always. He pressed everything into His service. He drew His figures from the most familiar objects around Him.* From the undulating cornfield with its hard trodden pathway, and the rocky ground protruding here and there from the hillside, and the thorns springing up and over-shadowing the wheat; from the shepherd leading his flocks, and the busy fisherman plying his nets, and the shoals of fish of various kinds; from the countless flocks of birds flying in the air, and the lilies resplendent with a beauty to which Solomon in all his glory could not be compared;—from all these He "took up His parable," borrowing His illustrations alike from the world of nature and the world of men.

We too have our twofold debt, to the poor and to the rich, to the untaught as well as the instructed; for "the Apostle's broad divisions still part society, and run through it in its most remote portions."† But we are apt to forget our duty to the poor, and to confound preaching to the poor with poor preach-ing. The precise opposite of this is required in dealing with them. With them we are bound to be more than careful, and for their sakes to be especially patient and painstaking. We must grave upon our minds the thought that behind "the dim and hampered intellect," to which we find it so hard to get near, lies the soul, open to the secret operation of divine Grace, open to deep convictions, open to the touch of sympathy. And if we would work

* See Stanley's *Sinai and Palestine*, p. 427.
† Dean Church's *Human Life, &c.*, p. 148.

with our Lord in a work of which, though out of
sight, He takes the chief share, we must remember
how He left nothing undone in His efforts to make
great truths understood by the meanest capacity.*
We are bound to remember our debt to the poor,
to take thought for them, to sympathize with them,
to make their interests ours, even as the Good
Shepherd ever did. But just as there is a tendency
to evade the debt we owe to the poor and un-
instructed, so there is a still greater tendency to
evade that which we owe to intellectual power and
reach of mind. Here, again, our Lord's example
is full of instruction. He Who had His message
for the Galilean boatmen, had His message also
for the cultivated, enquiring Greeks, for those
" strangers from the West." He had His explanation of the Philosophy of the Cross in the seed-corn
" cast into the ground and dying "† before it " could
bring forth fruit." And what He did St. Paul did
likewise, " making himself all things to all men,"
bringing out of his treasure alike for philosophers
at Athens and Roman governors at Cæsarea
"things new and old." And if we would at all
follow the example of the Apostle, we must like
him realize the vast range and majestic sweep of
the *Bibliotheca Divina*, the Divine Library of Holy
Scripture. We must strive to see in the sacred

---

* " The Lord's ' poor,' the poor in material resources, the poor in intellec-
tual endowments, the poor, I will add, in moral capacities and
attainments, are committed to the charge of the Christian Minister.
For him men, this man and this, are beings ' for whom Christ shed
His blood,' whom ' He has bought with His death.' " Bishop
Westcott's *Thoughts from the Ordinal*, p. 45.

† John xii. 20—26.

history of the discipline of the world the largeness
of the mode of God's action. We must ponder the
manifestations of His love, of His patience, of His
long-suffering, sometimes even startling to our eyes.
We must learn to trace, if with aching sight, how
He makes man minister to man, and race to race,
and generation to generation; how He accepts in
compassion varieties of service according to the
state and means of those who render it; how He
can turn to a source of blessing what appears to
our eyes simple misery and ruin.* It is an important question how far we are trying to recognise
our twofold debt, how far we are endeavouring to
show ourselves "approved money-changers," not
talking, but thinking, as we ought to think, of our
great trust and our Ministry to the wise as well
as the unwise.

And here we may well consider a few golden
rules respecting the adequate discharge of the prophetical office. And first one golden rule laid
down by the late Bishop Wilberforce deserves
attention. "To secure thought and preparation,"
he says, "begin, whenever it is possible, or at all
events choose the subject of next Sunday's sermon
at least on the preceding Monday."† Let it be
turned over and over again in your mind; and,

---

* Bishop Westcott's *Thoughts from the Ordinal*, pp. 20, 21.

† "Think your subject thoroughly over; settle, if possible on Sunday
evening, next Sunday's subject. Meditate on it as you walk about
your parish; pray for power to enforce it; and as you read God's
Word, and go about your parish, light will break out on it, illustrations occur, applications suggest themselves; and when you write
or speak, you will be full and orderly, and this is to be strong."
Bishop Wilberforce's *Ordination Addresses*, p. 14.

remember, patient labour is essential to secure for
the sermon depth, solidity, and order. It is mainly
idleness which ruins sermons, which makes them
vague, confused, powerless, and dull. The saying
is a caustic one, but nevertheless it is true, " the
sermon which has cost little, is worth just what it
cost."

If it is asked what *order* should be observed
in preaching, happily there can be no difficulty
about answering the question. The order of the
Church's Seasons is the order we are bound to
follow. No man, if he desires to be faithful to his
Prayer Book, would dream of ignoring the Fasts
and Festivals of the Church as they come round,
and the events commemorated by them. The
Church's Seasons lead us past all the great events
in the life of our Blessed Lord in their due suc-
cession, and provide subjects for the most ample
variety of teaching. " I am sure I rejoice," says
the late Bishop Brooks in some lectures delivered
before the Divinity School of Yale College, " to
see in many Churches outside our own, that to
which we owe so much as a help in the orderliness
of preaching, viz., the observance of the Church's
year, as it comes round with its commemorative
Festivals, growing so largely common. It is no
bondage, within which any man is hampered. It
still leaves the largest liberty. The great procession
of the year, sacred to our best interests, with its
accumulated reverence of ages—Advent, Christmas,
Epiphany, Good Friday, Easter, Ascension, Whit-
sunday—leads those who walk in it, at least once

every year, past all the great Christian facts, and however careless and selfish be the preacher, will not leave it in his power to keep them from his people."* This is a remarkable testimony as to the debt owing by the New to the Old World, and well describes the privilege we enjoy as members of the Church of England in the due recurrence of of the Church's Seasons.

And here it is natural to ask, "should sermons be written or unwritten?" The answer does not admit of much hesitation. Write certainly at first, and indeed for some considerable time after commencing your ministry. "I myself," said that great master of pulpit eloquence, the late Bishop Wilberforce, "preached written sermons for fifteen years after my Ordination." In writing it is well by a system of introduction, theme, and conclusion, to secure proportion and clearness. The introduction should not be too long; it should be kept within due bounds, lest it become "all porch;" and it should lead without delay to the theme which it is wished to expound; and the conclusion should be confined to one or two points, and have for its aim the enforcing of the subject on the will and the affections so as to lead to action. The sentences should be pithy and short, and the words plain and simple; the abstract should give way to the concrete; and it is well if the sermon can be written off at a heat, while the heart is warm and the thoughts flow without impediment. To these a few homely hints may be added. Let the MS. be written well and large; let the writing be on one side only, the

* Bishop Brooks' *Lectures on Preaching*, p. 91.

D

right side; let the different paragraphs be distinctly marked off the one from the other; and above all let the MS. be read over three or four times before the sermon is preached, so that there will be then no necessity for the eye to be glued to the page, but helped to look from the written page to the audience that is to be addressed. The freedom of the eye in preaching is a point of great importance.

But method and system are equally necessary, nay even more necessary for unwritten sermons. The man, who possesses the fatal gift of natural fluency, is apt to trust to the occasion, and to let a torrent of words make up for reading and thought. The present Archbishop of Canterbury said once at a Clerical Meeting in the Diocese of Exeter, "Write your sermon. Burn it. Write it again. Burn it. Then preach it." The effort implied would be very great, but it is noticeable how much stress is laid upon the writing. This is essential, and when from writing out a full MS. a man can feel himself able to depend simply on notes, let them be carefully and methodically arranged, with the important words and sentences clearly under-lined, that the eye, which is the chief handmaid of the memory, may the more easily recall them, and help to an effective delivery. But it is well to avoid trying to learn a sermon by heart and to repeat it from recollection. The effort is painful alike to the preacher and to the hearers. It is better far to carefully prepare the notes, and to trust to the occasion and the divine help, which of course will be invoked, to supply the actual words, which will thus come more directly from the heart of the preacher to the hearts of his people.

There is one style of sermons which is too much neglected, but which is of especial value, and that is expositional sermons, or explanations of large consecutive portions of Holy Scripture. This was the style adopted by nearly all the early Fathers, by St. Ambrose, St. Chrysostom, St. Augustine, the Venerable Bede and others. Till the experiment has been made, the newly ordained minister can form no idea how little most people know of Holy Scripture, how little able they are of themselves to follow and understand and apply a parable, or a miracle, or an argument in St. Paul's Epistles, or even the Sermon on the Mount. Sermons are far too exclusively hortatory in their character. Men and women whose weeks are weeks of exhausting labour, and many who belong to the higher and better instructed classes, need not only to be urged and exhorted to Christian living, but also and especially to be *taught*. They require to learn how to read their Bibles, how to apply them, how to communicate, how to pray, how to examine themselves; and on all these points expositions of consecutive portions of Scripture afford many opportunities of giving the instruction required, and an experiment has only to be made to learn its value. Not the least of its advantages is that by the expositional system you have the assurance that you are "teaching," premonishing, feeding the flock committed to your charge from the very Word of God Himself.

Whether a sermon be written or unwritten, its efficiency depends on delivery. The preacher speaks to his people *ut doceat, ut delectet, ut flectat*. But he can do none of these things unless his delivery be marked by (1) clearness and (2) earnestness.

(1)—*Clearness.* The great thing to avoid is anything that savours of self-consciousness, pomposity, or affectation. The sermon should be delivered in a distinct tone, every word should be properly sounded, the pronouns and conjunctions should receive particular attention, and the preacher, instead of being hurried, should be moderately deliberate and should know when to pause. Young preachers are too often in a state of breathless haste to come to a conclusion, and the hearers lose much by being hurried from point to point. If the sermon has been read over carefully beforehand, the preacher will not need to keep his eyes fixed on the MS., but will be able to preach off it, as if it hardly lay before him at all. This reading over beforehand is not always sufficiently attended to, but it makes all the difference towards securing an easy and effective delivery.

(2)—*Earnestness.* Earnestness does not mean rant, or noise, or a declamatory style. It means that in his inmost soul he feels what he has to say, and is not ashamed to feel it, and let others see that he feels it. Earnestness must not be confounded with emotionalism. As a rule English people are not naturally emotional. They have a very decided tendency to reserve, especially

in regard to religious matters. Moreover it is
to be remembered that the emotions are too often
evanescent in their effects. People can " be quickly
moved because not deeply moved," and need to be
cautioned against putting trust in frames and feelings. No sermons in their day ever exerted greater
effect than those of John Henry Newman, when he
was Vicar of St. Mary's, Oxford. It was impossible
to resist the tone and manner in which they were
delivered. But there was no excitement about them,
no mere emotionalism. " There was not very much
change in the inflexion of his voice," writes Mr.
Gladstone; " action there was none....but there
was a stamp and seal upon the man, there was a
solemn sweetness and music in the tone, which
made even his delivery singularly attractive." " No
one who has heard his sermons," writes Mr. J. A.
Froude, " can ever forget them....He seemed to be
addressing the most secret consciousness of each of
us, as the eyes of a portrait appear to look at every
person in the room. He was never exaggerated;
he was never unreal. Once he was describing
some of the incidents of our Lord's Passion;
then he paused. For a few moments there was
a breathless silence. Then in a low, clear voice,
of which the faintest vibration was audible in the
furthest corner of St. Mary's, he said, 'Now, I bid
you recollect that He, to Whom these things were
done, was Almighty God.' It was like as if an
electric shock had gone through the church, as if
every person present understood for the first time
the meaning of what he had all his life been saying."
In Newman's style there was true earnestness. But

it was not excitement or mere emotionalism. It was
reality.*

But side by side with earnestness the preacher
ought to evince *sympathy with his people*. This
feature especially marked the preaching of "the
Shepherd of Shepherds." When He opened His
mouth to address the multitudes on the Mount, He
uttered not a commandment, or a philosophy, but
a beatitude. And He had His blessed words of
sympathy for little children, whom their mothers
placed in His arms; for the grief-stricken house-
hold of Jairus; for the lonely widow of Nain; for
the suffering woman, who grasped the hem of His
robe; for the sorrow-stricken sisters of Lazarus.
Nay, on one occasion He broke forth in His divine
compassion, "O Jerusalem, Jerusalem, which killeth
the prophets and stoneth them that are sent
unto her! how often would I have gathered thy
children together, even as a hen gathereth her
chickens under her wings, and ye would not!"†
Tenderness, sympathy accompanied the delivery of
His message to men. And even so love for our
people should accompany "the solemn delivery of
the burden of the Lord," lest we mingle strange
fire with the flame from the holy Altar.‡ "We
should strive to feel what St. Paul felt, when he said,

* " Only when the soul goes forth out of itself, and speaks to the soul, can
man sway the will of man. Eloquence then is all soul, embodied, it
may be, in burning, forceful words, but with a power above the power
of words, an electric force, which pierces the soul addressed, transposes
into it another's thoughts, making them its own, by going forth out of
itself." Pusey's *University Sermons*, 1859—72, p. 7.

† Matt. xxiii. 37.

‡ Bridges' *Christian Ministry*, p. 355.

as one to whom the task of the preacher had been committed, "the love of Christ constraineth us," " as ambassadors we beseech you on behalf of Christ, be ye reconciled to God,"* "knowing the fear of the Lord we persuade men."† But the tenderness of the Good Shepherd did not evaporate into mere emotionalism or sentimentality. He feels deeply for the anxious enquirer who comes to him by night, but He does not spare him the staggering assertion that he must " be born again."‡ He looks upon the rich young ruler and loves him, but bids him, if he would be perfect, sell all that he has and give to the poor.§ He feels for men as no one ever felt before, but He ever seeks to make them stronger, deeper, and more spiritual, not sparing, when necessary, His "hard sayings." We cannot do exactly what He did. But at any rate we can see that our sympathy does not err by excess. We can aim at being manly as well as sympathetic, strong as well as loving, realizing in ourselves more and more what is meant by speaking from the soul to the soul for its eternal welfare.

But with tenderness there must ever be *boldness*. The "Shepherd of Shepherds" was full of boldness. With what stern incisiveness, with what terrible severity He could denounce the leaders of the nation ! Seven times‖ we find Him, in the warnings He addresses for the last time during Holy Week to

---

* II Cor. v. 14, 20.

† II Cor. v. 11. " The soul and brain of St. Paul are so conspicuous, that
   we are apt to forget and ignore the glow and tenderness of his heart."
   Bishop Gott's *Parish Priest of the Town*, p. 98.

‡ John iii. 3.   § Mark x. 21.   ‖ Matt. xxiii. 13, 15, 16, 23, 25, 27, 29.

the rulers of the nation, repeating the terrible words,
"Woe unto you, scribes and Pharisees, hypocrites!"
Ten times He denounces the hypocrisy, the hollow-
ness, the pretence of the high religious professors
of the day. "Blind guides,"* "fools and blind,"
"whited sepulchres," "an evil generation," "an
evil and adulterous generation,"—these are some
of the expressions which He used respecting the
men of His generation, setting His face as a
flint, and caring nothing for the passions of men.
Boldness is essential from time to time. There are
the cowardices of the social table, the cowardices
of the fire-side and the market-place, but there is
also the cowardice of the pulpit. Fear of running
counter to the world's opinion, fear of speaking out,
fear of saying what may be misapprehended, has
weakened the utterances and frittered away the influence of many a preacher of the Word. Such
tremulous timidity makes men think we are only
half-believers in our great commission, and paralyzes
our real influence. There is of course a time to be
silent, but there is also a time to speak, though
it must be done with prudence and judgment. "Am
I seeking to please men?" asks St. Paul.† The
desire to please men is a great snare. It is this,
which, as it has been remarked, constitutes the deep
and fatal flaw in the character of Lord Bacon. He
was a pleaser of men. "There was in him," says
Dean Church, "that subtle fault, noted and named
both by philosophy and religion in the ἄρεσκος of
Aristotle and the ἀνθρωπάρεσκος‡ of St. Paul, that is

* Matt. xxiii. 16, 24.   † Gal. i. 10.
‡ Eph. vi. 6; Col. iii. 22.

more common than it is pleasant to think of even
in good people, but which, if it becomes dominant
in a character, is ruinous alike to truth and power."*

Now it is just this wish to stand well with
men, to be popular, to be liked, which proves the
besetting sin of not a few in Holy Orders. The
tendency to dilute the messages, to trim the sails
to the varying wind, to purchase peace at any price,
is a great temptation, and needs great watchfulness
to guard against it. If there is one consideration
more than another which ought to come back with
all possible force to the commissioned pastors of
Christ's flock, it is that the deed which through
eighteen centuries has remained the great indictment
against humanity—the condemnation of our Lord
to death—was brought about by the fact that the
members of the Jewish Sanhedrim, though many of
them believed in Him,† would not openly confess
Him, because they loved the praise of men more
than the praise of God ;‡ and also by the fact that
Pilate, who had the most signal opportunity of
releasing Him, on hearing the crafty cry, "If thou
let this man go, thou art not Cæsar's friend,"§
through fear of man pronounced the irrevocable
words "let Him be crucified."‖ And if there is a
prayer, which, more earnestly than another, the
shepherd of Christ's flock on earth ought to put up,
it is one to be found in the Devotions of that

* Dean Church's *Life of Bacon*, pp. 3, 4.

† Ὅμως μέντοι καὶ ἐκ τῶν ἀρχόντων πολλοὶ ἐπίστευσαν εἰς αὐτόν.
John xii. 42.

‡ John xii. 43.   § John xix. 12.   ‖ Matt. xxvii. 26 ; Mark xv. 15.

Bishop Andrewes to whom Bacon submitted all his works, and whom he called his inquisitor-general :—

> "From the fear of man,
> From the love of human approbation,
> From shrinking from any unpleasant duty,
>   Good Lord, deliver us."

CHAPTER VI.

OUR LORD'S ZEAL FOR THE HONOUR OF HIS FATHER'S HOUSE.

Few events in the ministry of our Lord seem to have made a greater impression on St. John than that which signalized the first Passover of his Master's public ministry. Just returned from the marriage-feast at Cana, He joined the Paschal company* in their journey southward towards Jerusalem, and in the Temple was confronted with the scene of desecration which had converted, if not the sanctuary, at least the outer court, into a wrangling mart, where nothing was to be heard save the noisy huckstering of traders recommending their wares.†

No sooner however did His eye rest upon the scene than His righteous anger displayed itself. Fashioning a scourge of the rushes‡ that strewed the ground, He drove forth the sheep and the oxen;

* Καὶ ἐγγὺς ἦν τὸ πάσχα τῶν Ἰουδαίων. John ii. 13.

† John ii. 14.

‡ Φραγέλλιον ἐκ σχοινίων.

He overthrew the tables of the money-changers;* He found out their unholy gains, and bade those even who sold doves, to take these things hence, and make not "His Father's house" a house of merchandise.

Awed by the look, the tone, the calm majesty of the Redeemer, the desecrators quitted the scene of their mercenary traffic, and a silence reigned around, which had been long unknown. Two years later† however things had become as bad, if not worse. Therefore He once more performed this act of cleansing, but without using any scourge, and affirming on this latter occasion that the desecrators, who before had made His Father's house a "house of merchandise," has now made it a "den of robbers,"‡ a "bandits' cave." The first cleansing had been a sign and a warning, the second a judicial sentence, a symbol of "the wrath of the lamb"§ in its terrible and consuming power.

Thus did the great High Priest vindicate the dignity and sacredness of His Father's house, and twice defend the honour due to material structures consecrated to the worship of God. Now if our ministry is far above the ministry of the Jewish priesthood; if the veil, which separated their Holy Place from the Most Holy, has for ever been rent

---

* Note the touch of an eye witness in τοὺς κερματιστὰς καθημένους.

† Matt. xxi. 12—13; Mark xi. 15—18; Luke xix. 45—48.

‡ Σπήλαιον λῃστῶν. These words are preserved by all the Synoptists. Λῃστής is not a thief, a secret purloiner, but a bandit, a brigand, who acts by violence and openly. Comp. II Cor. xi. 26, κινδύνοις λῃστῶν.

§ Ἡ ὀργὴ τοῦ ἀρνίου. *Ira agni.* Vulg. Rev. vi. 16.

in twain,* and we can enter where they of the Jewish priesthood could not; if they came to God in typical sacrifices, and the Son of God comes to us in effectual sacraments; what manner of men ought we to be in our daily ministrations? As representatives of our people, with a definite ministry, definite places of worship, definite means of grace, definite fasts and festivals, how much of awe and reverence ought to enter into the performance of our sacred functions! If our Lord demanded respect for the external ἱερόν, dedicated to the Most High, does He not demand still more of those who are called to minister in the ναός, the sanctuary, the Holy of Holies?

"Sanctus sancte sancta tractat." The High Priest of the Jewish Dispensation was never allowed to appear before God in the discharge of his sacred ministry without wearing a plate of pure gold fastened to his mitre by blue braids,† and inscribed with the solemn words, "Holiness to the Lord." Can we expect that less reverence and "godly fear" is required by the same Lord of us, to whom has been entrusted the ministration of a better Covenant? If the ministration of "the letter" was glorious, ought not the ministration of the spirit to exceed in the glory of the consecrated lives of those who are its ordained ministers? What does the Bishop ask of us at our ordination to the diaconate?—

"Will you apply all your diligence to frame

---

* Matt. xxvii. 51.   † Exod. xxviii. 36—39 ; xxxix. 30.

and fashion your own lives....according to the Doctrine of Christ?"

What does he ask of those who have obtained the right to the higher step of the priesthood?—

" Will you be diligent to frame and fashion your *own selves*....according to the Doctrine of Christ?"

" Sanctus sante sancta tractat." The ability to handle holy things holily depends on the complexion of the inward life. Every age of the Church attests the terrible results of an unholy, immoral, corrupt priesthood. What made Israel in the days of Eli "abhor the offering of the Lord"? Was it not the lives, so scandalously corrupt, of Hophni and Phinehas?* What made Cyprian tremble for the Church of Carthage, so that he declared that the winnowing fan of persecution would be a mercy and not a judgment? Was it not the loose and careless lives of the clergy? What filled Hugh of Lincoln and Robert Grosseteste in the middle ages with such fear for the future of the Church and such indignation against the things that went on around them? Was it not the unholy lives of "the Messengers, the Watchmen, the Stewards of the Lord"? What made it necessary to introduce a special Article amongst our own Thirty-nine on the " Unworthiness of the Ministers, which hinders not the effect of the Sacrament"? Was it not because the lives of many of the clergy made them a by-word amongst their people, because they had well-nigh

* I Sam. ii. 17.

ceased " to consider the end of their Ministry towards the children of God, towards the Spouse and Body of Christ " ? Because the greed of gain, which set up the dove-cotes of Annas and the exchangers' stalls of Caiaphas in the courts of the Temple at Jerusalem, had re-appeared amongst the highest of the Curia of the Vicar of Christ ? Was it not this, together with the traffic in pardons and indulgences, which in a great measure precipitated, what had long been threatened, the revolt of the Teutonic races in the sixteenth century ?*

Other things may be dispensed with, but personal piety, personal consecration, cannot be dispensed with. This is the uniform teaching of a Chrysostom in his " Treatise on the Priesthood " ; of a Gregory in his work "De Sacerdotio"; of a George Herbert in his " Country Parson " ; of a Burnet in his " Pastoral Care"; of a Jeremy Taylor in his most solemn charges ; of a Bridges in his " Christian Ministry " ; of a Heygate in his " Ember Hours." But this is exactly what those in Holy Orders are tempted to forget. Rightly said a layman once to a parish priest, " My danger is that of making my business my God, yours is of making your God your business." To nothing indeed are men more prone than to lower the standard of personal consecration, and to think that if they are respectable enough to serve as a pattern, it does not so much matter if it is a very easy pattern.

* " An ignorant Clergy is a reproach to any Church, and must injure its efficiency ; but an ungodly Clergy threatens the removal of its candle-stick, and the extinction of its life." Bishop Wilberforce, *Ordination Addresses*, p. 1.

And if it is true that it is difficult to avoid easiness of living, a careless self-indulgence, an indolence constitutional or acquired, it is true also that in many there is a tendency to forget the necessity for carefulness in handling holy things, and in discharging the various duties of the sacred office of the Christian minister. What is the literal meaning of the adjective εὐλαβής,* which we so often find connected in the New Testament with sacred functions? Is it not carefulness in handling some precious vase or chalice, then carefulness in religious rites, and so religious awe generally? Now this is exactly the spirit which becomes the Christian deacon and priest. In the discharge of his sacred functions there ought to be a deep sense of the presence of God.

It is well in the vestry, before the service begins, to realize what it is we are about to engage in,† and to whom we are about to minister. We cannot expect the choir, whether men or boys, to preserve a reverent spirit, if they see him, who is about to take the service, careless and indifferent. In saying Matins and Evensong it is ever needful to remember the words, " Before thou prayest prepare thyself, and be not as one that tempteth the Lord;"‡ and in pronouncing the words of Absolution to ask

---

* Εὐλάβεια marks that "careful watchfulness, which pays regard to every circumstance in the rite, with which the celebrant has to deal." Bishop Westcott on Heb. v. 7.

† "The daily Matins and Evensong will scarcely reach the height of a Divine Service, unless some kind of procession of the soul takes place from our Vestry to our Prayer Desk." Bishop Gott's *Parish Priest,* pp. 178, 179.

‡ Ecclus. xviii. 23.

pardon in silent prayer for ourselves, before we
pronounce the pardon of God over our people.
Would not the habit of repeating such a form as—
"Munda cor meum et labia mea, Omnipotens Deus,"
be a suitable preparation for so solemn a function?
Moreover it is well to avoid reading the Lessons
without preparation, and to remember the custom
of the late Bishop Wordsworth of Lincoln:—"Rarely,
if ever," we are told, "did he read the Lessons,
even in his own chapel at Riseholme, without first
going through them and meditating on them in
private."*

Above all in the ministration of the Sacraments it is essential to remember that "Reverence,
Reverence, Reverence" is the body, soul, and spirit†
of him who celebrates. Who is worthy, with his
manifold shortcomings, to consecrate the water at
the baptismal font, until he has silently acknowledged the grace of Him Who permits him to act
on the command of that ascended Lord, Who by
His "outward gesture and deed" declared His
good will towards little children, "and took them up
into His arms and blessed them." And as regards
the celebration of the Holy Eucharist, it is impossible to be too careful in securing time for
adequate preparation, examining ourselves, and
passing in review the many who hang on our
intercession, or for whom we are in private duty
bound to pray, before we take our part in the
central and supreme act of the Christian Ministry,

---

* Bishop John Wordsworth's *Memorial Sermon*.
† See Bishop Gott's *Parish Priest of the Town*, p. 180.

E

by which it is directly associated with His media-
torial work in heaven. That is a truly appropriate
prayer which the late Bishop Armstrong gives in
his little book entitled "The Pastor in his Closet:"—
"Assist me, heavenly Father, for Thy dear Son's
sake, especially in the more solemn parts of my
ministrations. Assist me, most merciful Saviour,
especially when I minister Thy Holy Sacraments.
When I administer Holy Baptism, may I do it with
a devout will, with faith, with sincere prayer.
When I administer the Holy Eucharist, take me,
as it were, out of the world; shut the gate of my
heart against it; lift up my spirit; may I feel
myself to be on holy ground. I cannot draw nearer
to Thee on earth. Grant that I may feel Thy
nearness unto me." Nor can we be surprised to
find in the diary of the late Bishop Wilberforce
such a sentence as this, "Let me secure retirement
before great occasions, *e.g.*, Consecrations, Ordina-
tions, Synods; let me remember the seclusion of the
Aaronic priesthood, before clothing in holy vesture."

And then as regards the Occasional Offices,
there is often a great danger of entering upon them
in a professional, perfunctory spirit.* When the
Christian priest catechizes, or celebrates a marriage,
or visits the sick, or buries the dead—in which has
he not to guard against lukewarmness and even
carelessness? For which office is not preparation

---

* "To marry groups of careless couples, to baptize noisy children by the
dozen in the presence of godless god-parents, to bury the dead day
after day without losing one's sympathy with those who mourn, and
one's own real and grave thoughts that help to make oneself ready to
die; these offices need special grace, if they are to be deeds of life and
means of grace." Bishop Gott's *Parish Priest*, p. 184.

needed that it may be used as a means of grace for
the priest himself, as a service to God, and an
occasion of sympathy with and ministering to
others? Never perhaps are greater opportunities
offered to the priest of doing permanent good than
in the visitation of the sick and in the chamber of
death. Even when we have for the last time conveyed to failing lips the Body and Blood of Him
Who is "the Resurrection and the Life," and the dark
shadows have closed around, and the spirit has
"returned to Him Who gave it," and the prayer of
commendation has sped its departure, even then
there is much that can be done. When the heads
of the mourners are bowed with grief, their sorrow
can be soothed by joining in prayer for him or her
who has been taken hence, and commending all in
prayer to the tender mercy and protecting care of
Him in Whose hands are the issues of life and
death.

The more completely the minister of Christ
throws himself with all his powers and faculties into
the discharge of his sacred functions, the more he
displays tact and thoughtfulness in everything he
does, or proves his power of sympathy with his
people in joy and sorrow; the more he will realize
to them the meaning of the lower part of the High
Priest's dress as prescribed to Moses in the divine
picture book of the Holy Mount. What was the
High Priest directed to wear on the fringe of
his ephod? A golden bell and a pomegranate.*
What was symbolized by these? Did not the golden

* Exod. xxviii. 33, 34.

bell symbolize the glad sound of his continued activity in service and intercession for his people? Did not the pomegranate, the emblem of fertility, symbolize his fruitfulness in good works? And does this apply less to the ministers of a better Covenant? It is not surprising that St. Jerome says, "Everything the priest does must have its message:—his life, his words, his actions." We do not estimate sufficiently the extent to which each of us possesses and exercises an influence,* an *influxus* or *influentia* of our lives into the lives of others. It is a fundamental fact of our being that we touch and attract, or harden and repel others in a way at once subtle and effectual. Two instances are to hand. It is recorded in the life of George Herbert that "the people did so love and reverence him that they would let their plough rest when Mr. Herbert's bell rang to prayers, that they might also with him offer their devotions to God, and then return back to their plough." And it is said that nothing at Hursley exercised such an influence over the people as the sight of Mr. Keble making his way through the snow at 5.30 a.m. to Hursley Church to say the Litany on Wednesdays and Fridays with a few labourers before their morning work, as reverently and devoutly as though he had been surrounded by a crowded congregation in a fashionable church.

---

* " The acts which we do directly to set an example, and the words which we speak to enforce it, are comparatively few and powerless when set beside the multitude of daily acts, looks, and words affecting others, which, as I said at first, are always flowing forth on others from our spiritual and moral being. Our real influence on them for good depends on the spiritual efficacy of this perpetual, unconscious exhibition and imparting of ourselves to them." Bishop Wilberforce's *Ordination Addresses*, p. 210.

A golden bell and a pomegranate. The golden
bell, however, must not sound intermittently, but
continuously. There must be consistent fruitfulness
in good works. "Semper idem" must be the
priest's motto. "He must not be," as a writer
quaintly says, "holy by fits and starts, now seething
hot in his profession, now lukewarm, then key-cold;
standing with Peter at the fire, then flying and
denying; good in thunder and lightning, or in a
storm at sea, while in ordinary life he is like other
men." At no time can he really say he is "off
duty." Intermittent uprightness, it has been said, is
as bad as intermittent fever. It weakens and dis-
appoints those who wish to have a living example
to follow. Whatever men may say, they *do* admire
consistency; and if they see a man walking ever in
a straight path, and setting an example alike in
his private and public life, they feel a respect for
him however much they may differ from his views.
Continuous consistency is strength.

A golden bell and a pomegranate. But the bell
must not sound harshly, and the pomegranate
must yield no bitter taste. It is remarkable how
often "joy" is dwelt upon in the Epistles as a mark
of the Christian character. Joy is one of the fruits
of the Spirit. A Christian priest is not called upon
to be sour-faced and sad, or to go through life as
if the east wind had entire possession of him. He is
not to be frivolous, or a jester, or a buffoon. Still
less is he intended to be a ministerial ice-berg. If
he believes that his sins are forgiven, that he is at
peace with God, that he is walking in the light,

there will be cheerfulness, serenity, joy in his demeanour. If he is walking in the sunshine, he cannot help reflecting the sunshine. Nothing commends our holy faith more than a consistent cheerfulness, a true sense of joy in believing. A man who is earnest yet not gloomy, truthful yet not hard, firm yet not unbending, cheerful yet not light, courteous and good humoured yet neither frivolous nor forward, possesses most of the qualities which, combined with a sense of holy fear in the discharge of his ministerial functions, will teach his people the true symbolism of "the golden bell and the pomegranate" of the High Priest of the Mosaic Dispensation. "Sanctus sancte sancta tractat." May He Who cleansed the ἱερόν of the Temple at Jerusalem grant us grace to cleanse the ναός of our souls in the service of His sheep!

CHAPTER VII.

OUR LORD'S ANXIETY FOR THE CONVERSION OF INDIVIDUAL SOULS.

Few incidents illustrate more strikingly our Lord's anxiety for the winning to Himself of individual souls than His interview with the woman of Samaria by the well of Sychar.

And first we cannot fail to notice the skill with which this great "fisher of men" prepared His angle to take this single soul.* Had it been a great multitude to be caught by one throw of His casting-net, we in our craving for results on a large scale should not have been surprised. But what is so wonderful is this, that He should have taken the journey through Samaria, and sat Him down, spent and weary on the well, and, when the woman came, should have devoted Himself to her case with as much solicitude as though no other being in the whole world needed His attention. This is so wonderful, and no less the merciful and tender consideration, wherewith He so ordered it,

* Trench's *Studies in the Gospels*, p. 91.

that, owing to the absence of His disciples,* there should be a solitude about Him, amidst which, free from all interruption, He could win her to repentance and through repentance to Himself.

The way moreover, in which He commences the interview when she comes, has been well called " a complete example of mission wisdom."† He begins by asking a service of her, "Give Me," He says, "to drink."‡ This removes prejudice and awakens attention. Besides it paves the way in the most natural manner for further conversation respecting many points—the relation between the Jews and the Samaritans, the depth and history of the well, the difference between its water and "the living water " which the Speaker claimed to be able to bestow.∥ This word of His respecting the living water leads to her request that it might be given to her, so that she need no more thirst, or come backwards and forwards to draw her supply from the depth of the well.§

Thus He has brought her to the point, where the profounder and personal teaching may begin. Apparently in a casual way, and without any hidden meaning, preparation or explanation, the Lord bids the woman " go, call her husband, and come hither."** This brings her to a sudden pause. " I have no husband," she stammers out.

---

* John iv. 8.   † Stier's *Words of the Lord Jesus.*

‡ Δός μοι πιεῖν. John iv. 7.   ∥ John iv. 9—14.

§ Δός μοι τοῦτο τὸ ὕδωρ, ἵνα μὴ διψῶ, μηδὲ διέρχωμαι ἐνθάδε ἀντλεῖν. John iv. 15.

** John iv. 16.

A truth, but not all the truth. For the stranger
proceeds to reveal His knowledge of the secret of
her inner life, how that after five lawful unions she
is now living in an illicit relation with one who
is "not her husband."* Instantly the whole tenour
of the conversation undergoes a change. She tries
to engage Him in a theological discussion on one
of the burning questions of the day. But He is
not to be turned from His purpose. Closer and
closer He draws near to her; and at last, when in
accordance with her Samaritan faith she remarks
that, when He comes, the Messiah would "declare
unto us all things,"† He lets fall the veil, which
has till now hidden Him from her, and He affirms,
"I that speak unto thee am He."‡

His end was gained. He had laid hold of this
woman's inner life. She, who had come to the
well with no serious thoughts or deep religious
convictions, is transformed into an eager herald of
the new-found Messiah. She leaves her pitcher,§
as the Apostles before had left their nets; and
deeming her original errand of no moment, she
hurries into the town to bid her friends and neigh-
bours come and see a man who had told her all
that ever she did. Thus did the Great Fisher lay
His angle for that single soul. Thus did this unknown woman, whose name has not been revealed

---

* John iv. 18.

† Ὅταν ἔλθῃ ἐκεῖνος, ἀναγγελεῖ ἡμῖν πάντα. John iv. 25.

‡ Ἐγώ εἰμι, ὁ λαλῶν σοι. John iv. 26.

§ Ἀφῆκε τὴν ὑδρίαν αὐτῆς. John iv. 28. "Recepto in cor Christo
Domino, quid faceret, nisi jam hydriam dimitteret, et evangelizare
curreret?" St. Aug. *Tract. in Johann.*

to us, become the first of many multitudes, who could apply to their case—what first applied to hers—the touching line of the *Dies Iræ*,

"Quærens me sedisti lassus."

If this incident stood alone, it would be suffi-cient to illustrate the care of the Good Shepherd for individual souls. But it has other parallels. As He dealt with her, so He dealt with Nico-demus,* when he came to Him under cover of night. So did He deal with the man whom He healed at the Pool of Bethesda, searching for him in the courts of the Temple, and letting fall words of warning as regards his future life.† So did He deal with the woman who, having an issue of blood, pressed through the crowd to touch the hem of His garment—stopping, turning, looking round upon the throng; till she, who had touched Him, came trembling and told Him all the truth.‡ So did He deal with Zacchæus, acknowledging at their full value his expedients to get a sight of Himself from the branches of the sycomore tree, inviting Himself to his house,§ sympathizing with and helping his efforts to attain a higher life. So did He, after His resurrection, deal with Simon Peter, making a solitude about Himself on the world's first Easter Day, so that no one should hear the Apostle's stammering ackowledgment of his terrible fall. ‖ In each and all these instances we recognise certain characteristics, which mark the dealings of the Great Shepherd with individual souls.

* John iii. 1—21.   † John v. 14.   ‡ Mark v. 32, 33.   § Luke xix. 5.
‖ Luke xxiv. 34 ; I Cor. xv. 5.

And first, *He is always accessible.* He is ever
ready to render spiritual help, He may be weary
and thirsty at the well, but the moment the Samaritan
woman draws near, He is willing at once to sur-
render to her His noontide rest. He may be tired
after a day of many ministerial activities, but He
is quite ready to receive the anxious Nicodemus.
He lays aside all thought of Himself, and any
sense of His own necessities disappears in the joy
of winning one soul to Himself. It has been said
that an appropriate fresco for a Clergy House would
be " Nicodemus coming to our Lord by night."
Surely an equally appropriate one would be, " His
session with the woman of Samaria at the well."
The Good Shepherd was always accessible. Who
has not cause in the ministerial life to blame himself for just the opposite ? We come in perhaps
after our afternoon engagements. On the table lies
a note requesting us to go at once and see this
person in great trouble, or that person who has
met with a serious accident. Perhaps a pleasant
visitor is expected, or there is an invitation asking
us out for the evening, or we are really tired after our
afternoon's employment. Then comes the thought,
" Why go at once ? Will not to-morrow do as
well ?" The still small voice of conscience that bids
us go without delay is stifled, and fortunate indeed
will it have been for us, if we do not find that the
opportunity of doing anything effectual has passed
away altogether. Now the Good Shepherd was
ever ready to help at the moment that help was
required. He was ever ready, " instant in season
and out of season." "As soon as a soul to be won

comes to Him, His thirst becomes the opportunity for calling the wanderer to Himself."* It was the thought of this, we are told, that once came home with impressiveness to St. Francis de Sales. During a visitation tour in the snow mountains of his diocese, he found a shepherd, who, in trying to save one of his flock, had fallen over a precipice, and lay dead and frozen. "O my God," said he, "this poor shepherd sought his missing sheep with an ardour which the ice could not chill. Why am I so cold and careless in seeking the sheep for whom Thou wast willing to die? Why can I not be as accessible as Thou wast?"†

But again we notice *our Lord's patience with the woman's ignorance.* It must have been no ordinary trial to Him to listen to her that sultry afternoon, as she went on talking about her forefather Jacob, and the depth of the well, and the logical question whether Gerizim or Jerusalem was the proper place for worshipping God. But He bears with her, and lets her speak on, and listens to all she has to say, and gradually leads her on to the point He desired. Now it is not easy to act like this. It is easy enough to be pleasant and agreeable to those who receive us kindly, and are ready to listen to what we say. But to be gentle, considerate, and for-bearing with the cold, the hard, the ignorant—this is a very different thing. A tendency to be easily put out, to lose one's temper, to be impatient and hasty with the rough and ignorant, is a defect fatal

* See Stier's *Words of the Lord Jesus.* Trench's *Studies*, p. 90.
† *Precious Stones*, p. 121.

in the case of anyone, but ten times more fatal in one who has to deal with souls. These defects, unless wrestled with in early years, grow with advancing age, and tend to repel rather than to attract. The graces of μακροθυμία and χρηστοτής,* which St. Paul bids Timothy cultivate, these are all important in dealing with the anxious enquirer, or the shrinking candidate for Confirmation, or the timid communicant. This is a point well deserving of remembering, when difficult cases arise, where it is necessary to speak plainly and decidedly. A parish priest in Suffolk had once, we are told, to speak to a leading farmer in his parish on the subject of some immoral practices. He called to speak to the man about the matter, and saw by the man's look he was quite aware of the object of his visit. He had evidently braced himself up for the encounter. But when, instead of addressing him in words of stern reproof, he said that as a sinning man he desired to help a fellow-sinner, the man was quite overcome. And he who had resolved to knock his visitor down had he severely denounced his sinful conduct, was after no long interval brought to see the error of his ways, and lived to become a very right hand to his pastor in the parish.

But again we cannot fail to observe *how ready our Lord was to acknowledge all the good he could in the Samaritan woman.* Though He could unravel all the tangled skein of her life, yet He accepts her half-acknowledgment as though it lacked nothing. However much He would have her acknowledge

* I Tim. i. 16; II Tim. ii. 24, 25.

more, He takes what she gives Him, and does
nothing to discourage her. " In this," He replies
to her half-confession, "thou saidst well, 'I have
no husband'....this hast thou said truly."* All
that He can say to encourage, that He does say.
And as with her, so He deals with Nicodemus.†
He accepts his coming, though it is under cover of
night. He does not spurn him from Himself. So
again with the man whom He heals at the pool of
Bethesda. He gives his presence afterwards in
the Temple its full value.‡ He recognises in it a
good sign. "Herein," He seems to say, "thou hast
done well. Now I will give thee a word of warning
as regards thy future life." So even when He is
being nailed to His Cross, He seizes on the one
point He can plead in behalf of those who are
inflicting on Him this cruel outrage,—He places
between them and the Eternal Father their ignorance of what they did.§ Now here we have a point
for our guidance in dealing with individual souls,
with the conscience-stricken sufferer on his bed of
sickness, with the youth who longs to live a higher
life and comes to us for guidance, with the way-
ward returner from the sins of middle life. Here
responsibility is very great. So much depends on
wisdom, tact, judgment, patience. We ought to
remember our Lord's example and always try to

---

* John iv. 17, 18.   Καλῶς εἶπας....τοῦτο ἀληθὲς εἴρηκας.

† John iii. 2.

‡ Εὑρίσκει αὐτὸν ὁ Ἰησοῦς ἐν τῷ ἱερῷ. John v. 14. It does not
mean that He lights upon him there. The words imply that He sought
out the object of His mercy.

§ Luke xxiii. 34.

encourage, to give anything that can be commended
in one who comes to us its full value, and to use it
as a lever whereby to raise that soul. The force of
the words of the Litany ought never to be forgotten,
that God despiseth not "*the sighing* of a contrite
heart, nor *the desire* of such as be sorrowful." "The
needle of penitence," it has been said, "must pre-
cede the thread of Gospel consolation." True,
most true. But we must help the needle of
penitence to make its way. The desire after a
higher and better life is not a native of the human
heart. It is rather an exotic. It has been trans-
planted from heaven to earth. It comes from Him
Whose office it is "to give repentance unto His
people."* It is a tender, delicate plant. It will
bear no rough handling, no trifling, no discouraging.
Coldness, want of gentleness and consideration will
kill it. Therefore our duty is to be tender and
considerate, to make every allowance, to appraise at
the highest value every favourable feature in any
case. It is recorded of Bishop Patteson that his
longing when a boy was that he might one day be
a clergyman. But why? Not that he might become
a popular preacher, but that he might utter the
solemn and comforting words of the Absolution,
"He pardoneth and absolveth all them that truly
repent, and unfeignedly believe His holy Gospel."
Did not this betray the instinct of the true spiritual
helper? Did it not reveal the secret of his remarkable influence afterwards over the islanders of
the Southern Seas?

* Acts iii. 26; v. 31; xi. 18.

But our Lord's mode of dealing with the Samaritan woman teaches us another lesson in dealing with individual souls, and this is to "*be firm.*" Though He acknowledges all the good He could in her, He does not fail to utter the command, "Go, call thy husband." He does not spare Nicodemus the startling announcement, "Ye must be born again."* He does not hide from the man whom He has healed at the Pool of Bethesda, when He finds him in the Temple, the secret of his malady, the hidden canker of past sin.† He does not allow the woman with the issue of blood, who has laid her hand on the hem of His robe, to pass from Him without an open acknowledgment of her past misery and all she had done to obtain a cure.‡ He does not exempt the truly repentant Peter from the searching enquiry three times repeated, "Simon, son of John, lovest thou Me?"§ Thus while He is tender and considerate, He is thorough. While He encourages, He probes. His patience never degenerates into weakness. We are apt to forget how terribly stern He could be with those He loved most, how He could say to the self-same Peter, on whom He had declared He would found His Church, "Get thee behind me, Satan." With Him thoroughness ever went hand in hand with sympathy. He was never weak in His dealing with souls. "Speak the truth in love," it has been said. Yes. But "speak the truth." "This is a golden text," writes an American

* John iii. 7.

† Μηκέτι ἁμάρτανε. John v. 14. Noli peccare (Vulg.), *i.e.* no longer continue in sin. Comp. I John iii. 6, 9.

‡ Mark v. 33.   § John xxi. 15—17.

divine, "to put into the book where you keep the names of your people, when you plead for them before God." Sympathy without thoroughness makes a plausible pastor, but one whose hold on his people soon grows weak, and whose touch is seldom vigorous and strong. Thoroughness without sympathy makes the sort of man whom people say they respect, but to whom they will seldom go, and whom they seldom care to see coming to them. But where the two unite, I think there will be nothing that will surprise you more than to discover how certain their power is. It is a saying of St. Basil, "He who would love according to the love of Christ, must expect sometimes to grieve the object of his love."

But undoubtedly it is a matter of no little difficulty to unite sympathy with thoroughness. Especially in the case of the sick it is a great temptation to shrink from plain speaking, and to indulge instead in general, vague, religious conversation. "I am well aware," says Bishop Woodford, "that it requires a struggle to enter upon religious topics at all, a severer struggle still to pass from the general to particulars, to speak not of sin but of the sick man's own sin, to come, in fact, to close quarters in the spiritual warfare. On the other hand I also believe that our people are prepared for and yearn for a closer handling of their individual case than we are sometimes disposed to venture upon, and that often-times, when we have finished our prayer and have retired from the room, the sick person falls back with a sense of disappointment, as one who has looked for good and has been sent empty away."*

The good effect of a straight word in season is well illustrated by an incident recorded in the life of the great Bishop Wilberforce. On Easter Eve, 1873, two months before his sudden call, Bishop Wilberforce told the rector of Alverstoke the following facts:—"Some weeks ago, late in the evening, I received a message from a sick and dying woman, living at some distance in a cottage in Oxfordshire. I ordered my horse and started immediately. I went up to the chamber, and knew not who lay there. 'You know me not,' she said, 'but I knew you thirty years ago. When I was a girl, you visited me at Alverstoke, and you asked me if I would be confirmed. I hesitated and said 'No.' You would not leave me, however, but sat down and spoke to me and my young cousin who was staying with me. We had just before engaged to go to Porchester Castle on the following Saturday with two soldiers for a frolic. But we listened to your words, and you left us to consider our decision whether we would be candidates for the blessing promised to the confirmed. At last we said, 'We will give up Porchester, and be candidates for confirmation.' So we were taught by you and confirmed, and ever since that hour I have tried to keep my confirmation promises, and to live in the faith and love of Christians. Now I can die in peace.'" "She lifted up her languid body," said

* Woodford. *The Great Commission,* p. 76.

Then St. Philip* and St. Nathanael† join them; and
after being associated with the Lord for a short
space, and witnessing His power over nature, the
six are permitted to return for a time to their old
life and their former occupations. After a while
four are more definitely called from their fishing
boats on the Galilean Lake,‡ and one from the toll
house at Capernaum.§ When events rendered
necessary a more decided step—we notice again the
absence of all hurry or precipitation—one evening
the Lord retired to a spot in the mountain-range
of Galilee with His disciples, and continued till
day-break in prayer to God.‖ Then in the early
morning¶ He called to Him twelve out of the
general body of His disciples, and formally named
them His "Apostles."

It is impossible to imagine greater care exercised
in the selection of a body of helpers and agents.
All that careful scrutiny and earnest prayer could
do was done. The call of the Twelve was entirely
due to their Lord,** and having chosen them, He

* John i. 43, 44.   † John i. 45—51.
‡ Matt. iv. 18—22 ; Mark i. 16; Luke v. i.
§ Matt. ix. 9 ; Mark ii. 14; Luke v. 27.
‖ Καὶ ἦν διανυκτερεύων ἐν τῇ προσευχῇ τοῦ θεοῦ. "Magnum hoc
negotium inter Deum et Mediatorem." Bengel.
¶ Ὅτε ἐγένετο ἡμέρα. Luke vi. 13.
** Of this He reminds the Apostles again and again. "Did not *I* choose
you—the Twelve ? Οὐκ ἐγὼ ὑμᾶς τοὺς δώδεκα ἐξελεξάμην ;
John vi. 70, He asks them as they come forth from the synagogue at
Capernaum. "I know whom *I* chose," Ἐγὼ οἶδα οὓς ἐξελεξάμην,
He says after He has washed their feet in the upper room, John xiii. 18.
"Ye did not choose Me, I Myself chose you," He reminds them after
the institution of the Holy Eucharist. Οὐκ ὑμεῖς με ἐξελέξασθε,
ἀλλ' ἐγὼ ἐξελεξάμην ὑμᾶς. John xv. 16. The emphasis of the ἐγώ
in every one of these passages is very noticeable.

devoted from that day forward the greater part of
His time to their training and preparation for their
future work. He never was unmindful of them
amidst the busiest labours and the most exacting
employments. He demanded of them much, but
He gave them far more. He required of them that
they should lay aside all low and unworthy motives
and hold their lives at His service. But He gave
them in "full measure," "pressed down and running
over," a patience and a sympathy which nothing
could weary and nothing could exhaust.

The example thus set us is of priceless importance in our dealing with helpers in various
departments of parochial work. "Make their
choice," His voice seems to say to us, "a matter of
prayer. Select with care. But when selected, give
those who are chosen all the sympathy and help
you can." St. Paul, who mentions so often his
"helpers" and "fellow workers,"* seems to labour to
find words to enforce on Timothy the importance of
gentleness and consideration in dealing with the
helpers he had chosen.† A great master, we are
told, was once asked, "What is the first condition
of successful teaching?" "Patience," he replied.
"What is the second?" "Patience," he repeated.
"What is the third"? He paused, and then said,
"Sympathy."‡ Patience and sympathy with the
difficulties of others are essential to ministerial
success. The helpers of the parish priest may have

* Ἀντιλήψεις, I Cor. xii. 28. Συνεργοί, Phil. iv. 3.

† Timothy is to be ἤπιος, mansuetus διδακτικός, docibilis, πρᾶος, modes-
tus, ἀνεξίκακος, patiens. II Tim. ii. 24, 25.

‡ Liddon's *Easter Sermons*, vol. i., p. 278.

difficulties of their own which he never had; they
may have been denied opportunities which were
freely granted to him; they may be weighed down
with incumbrances to which he is an entire stranger;
and therefore he is bound to remember the duty of
patience and consideration in his dealings with
them. This especially applies to Sunday School
teachers. The task of teaching must never be represented as a light or easy one. The Good
Shepherd did not hide from His Apostles the
difficulties and opposition they must be prepared to
encounter. And even so the parish priest, if he is
wise, will not hide from his helpers in the Sunday
School the pains, earnestness, and devotion, which
the duty they have undertaken demands for its
adequate discharge. No pains, therefore, ought to
be grudged as regards the teachers' meeting. It
is the key of the position. It is the duty of the
parish priest to arrange with care the scheme of
yearly or half-yearly instruction; and it is also his
duty to see that it is explained to the teachers in a
methodical and systematic manner, if he does not
wish their teaching to become vapid, aimless, and
dull, and to merit many of the complaints that are
urged from time to time against the Sunday School
system.

The patience of our Lord, however, in training
His Apostles was exhibited as much towards the
least as towards the most conspicuous of the Apostolic body. Like David's band of heroes, the "Twelve"
contained its most striking, its less striking, and its
least striking representatives. They were few men,
but with diversities of gifts. Our Lord however

was as patient in His dealings with the least
conspicuous as with the Three, the flower and crown
of the Twelve. When, during the long conversation that ensued after the institution of the Holy
Eucharist, Judas, "not Iscariot," interposes with the
question, "Lord, what is come to pass that Thou
wilt manifest Thyself unto us, and not unto the
world?"* the question seems out of place at such a
time and in view of what was so shortly to come
to pass. But, though we have never heard of this
Apostle putting forward a remark before, the Lord
answers him as fully as if he had been Peter, the
man of rock himself. And what He does for him
He does for St. Philip, when he says, "Lord, show
us the Father, and it sufficeth us;"† and for St.
Thomas, when he remarks, "Lord, we know not
whither Thou goest; how know we the way?"‡
Now we are tempted to do just the opposite of
this. We are prone to measure out our sympathy and our patience in varying proportions; we
have our interesting and uninteresting scholars;
we are apt to show our preference for the brilliant
and clever, and to pass over the dull and slow.
But patience with a few favourites is not the patience
of Christ, and he, who tries to take Him for an
example, will be careful not to judge only by the
outward appearance, but to show patience towards
all alike.

Further in training His Apostles our Lord is not
unwilling to *teach the same lesson over and over again.*
Thus after He has uttered the parables of the
" Sower " and the "Tares," He does not decline to

* John xiv. 22.　　† John xiv. 8.　　‡ John xiv. 5.

go over them again, and explain their true and
hidden meaning.* And though He has often
taught His Apostles the lesson of humility, yet on
His last journey to Jerusalem, He does not shrink
from teaching it again.† He calls to Him the
Twelve, takes a little child into His arms,‡ and
holds it in His embrace, while He enforces once
more the lesson of true pre-eminence in His kingdom. Thus too after His resurrection, when St.
Thomas has refused to credit the fact from the lips of
others,§ He has patience with the honest doubter,
and addressing Himself to him in the Upper Room,
as though the Apostle alone were present, offers him
the evidence which he had craved.‖ Now we all
know how keen is the temptation to ride rough-shod
over another's difficulties, and to scoff at his
slowness of apprehension. "To be patient with
misapprehensions, even with folly; to condescend to
explanations, where they might be deemed super-
fluous; to make the best of all that is admitted in
the direction of truth; to appeal to the lower as
well as to the higher powers of the learner:—this,
it has been said, is to do as our Lord did—this
is to teach as He taught."¶ But how often we
notice the very opposite of this! "I have explained
all this to you before. I am tired of going over
the same ground again and again. It is so irksome
trying to repeat and repeat." Do we not know

* Matt. xiii. 18—23, 36—43; Mark iv. 10—20.
† Matt. xviii. 1; Mark ix. 35; Luke ix. 46.
‡ Καὶ ἐναγκαλισάμενος αὐτὸ εἶπεν αὐτοῖς.
§ John xx. 25. The negative οὐ μὴ πιστεύσω is expressed in its strongest
form. He says not, "If I see....I will believe;" but, "Except I see,
ἐὰν μὴ ἴδω, I will *in no wise* believe."
‖ John xx. 27.   ¶ Liddon's *Easter in St. Paul's.*

how easy it is to use words like these? Whenever we are so tempted, let us remember how He Who was "the Word," and "the Word was God," taught "line upon line," "precept upon precept," "here a little, and there a little."

Again we cannot but notice that our Lord's training of His Apostles was *gradual and progressive.* "I have many things to say unto you, but ye cannot bear them now:" thus He reminded them. And though He had to deal with men who could not possibly enter into the secret of His life, who could not give Him even "a cup of cold water" to testify their sympathy with the mystery of His Cross, yet He was never impatient, never hurried in His teaching. First He lays down in the Sermon on the Mount the laws of His kingdom. Then He proves Himself in ways they could not mistake supreme over nature, over the spirit world, over disease, over death. Then, when by His transfiguration He has revealed to them a glimpse of His inherent deity, and not till then, He begins to intimate clearly that He must suffer and must die. Order and method mark His hand in the world of nature. Order and method mark His wisdom as a teacher. His authoritative words and life-giving deeds carry with them to the minds of the Apostles the unmistakable conviction of a presence more than human. From love and admiration they pass on to awe and worship. Behind the manhood they discern the Godhead,* and gradually understand Him, when He claims to be the first of all, and the centre of all; when without any apology or

* See Liddon's *Bampton Lectures.*

explanation He proclaims Himself "the Light of
the world," the "Shepherd of the souls of men,"
"the Way, the Truth, and the Life," the one mode
and way of access to the Father.

And while His teaching is thus unmistakably
dogmatic, and all centres round and radiates from
Himself, how much of it is conveyed in a *catechetical
form*, by *question and answer*! A crucial instance
of this occurs at the middle point of His ministry,*
when He is anxious to ascertain from His Apostles
the result of the intercourse of so many days. As
an experienced teacher, before beginning a new
lesson, He makes them recapitulate the old. But
how does He begin? With a question, "Who do men
say that I the Son of man am?"† The question
excites an answer. What follows? A second question,
"But *ye*, who do *ye* say that I am?"‡ And this leads
to the full confession made in their name by St.
Peter, that He was "the Christ, the Son of the
living God."§ Again, when after His resurrection
He joins the despondent two journeying to Emmaus,
and wishes to teach them the lesson of Easter-Day,
how does He begin? Again it is with a question,

---

* "In the neighbourhood of Cæsarea Philippi, the very name of which place,
recalling as it did the foreign dominion of Cæsar, must have had a
depressing sound to the natural hopes and aspirations of patriotic
Jews." Gore's *Sermon in Westminster Abbey*.

† Matt. xvi. 13.

‡ Notice the emphatic ὑμεῖς Matt. xvi. 15—ὑμεῖς δὲ τίνα με λέγετε
εἶναι; On the opinion of the outer world He makes no comment.
They might speak of him vaguely as something wonderful and extra-
ordinary, without caring to examine more closely into His claims. But
of those who were to constitute His Church, of them deeper knowledge is required. So He presses the question to them closer home,
"Who do *ye* say that I am?" Gore's *Sermon in Westminster
Abbey*. St. Peter's Day, 1890. *Guardian*, July 2, 1890.

§ Σὺ εἶ ὁ Χριστός, ὁ υἱὸς τοῦ Θεοῦ τοῦ ζῶντος. Matt. xvi. 16.

" What communications are these that ye have one
with another, as ye walk ? "* And when they stand
looking sad and despondent, and one of them
enquires how He could be ignorant of what had
recently taken place in Jerusalem,† how does He
carry them a step further ? By another question,
" What things ? "‡ Then having elicited a precise
statement of their perplexities from their own
mouths, He proceeds to remove them, and to reveal
to them in all the Scriptures the things concerning
Himself."§

Now here surely we have a definite model and
warrant for the practice of catechetical teaching,
which has always held so distinguished a place
in the Church from the earliest times. Types of
such models of teaching we have in the *Pædagogue*
of St. Clement, A.D. 200, in the Catechetical
Lectures of St. Cyril of Jerusalem, A.D. 397, in
the *De Catechizandis Rudibus* of St. Augustine of
Hippo, A.D. 415, and in many other treatises. As
in many other particulars, so in the matter of
catechizing, the Reformation only rekindled a
primitive Catholic principle and practice. The
Injunctions framed by Cranmer in 1536 reiterated
the rule of earlier times that children should be
taught in their mother tongue the first principles
of the Christian Faith; and hence it is that we
have now our own Catechism, which has taught
so many generations of English men and English
women the Christian's covenant position, the Christ-

---

* Luke xxiv. 17.   † Luke xxiv. 17, 18. Καὶ ἐστάθησαν σκυθρωποί.

‡ Καὶ εἶπεν αὐτοῖς, Ποῖα ; Luke xxiv. 19.

§ Διηρμήνευσεν αὐτοῖς ἐν ταῖς γραφαῖς τὰ περὶ ἑαυτοῦ. Luke xxiv. 27.

ian's creed, the Christian's duty, the Christian's prayer, the Christian's sacraments.

But it must not be imagined that it is an easy thing to catechize properly. It has been said that "a boy can preach, but it takes a man to cate-chize." Though this may be somewhat of an exaggeration, it is undoubtedly true that it needs *special qualifications* to become a good catechist. Bishop King gave a list of them once in his Pastoral Lectures at Cuddesdon, which runs thus:—

i. *Knowledge.* You must *know* what you are going to teach.

ii. *Clearness.* You must be sure you can put forth clearly and systematically what you wish to say.

iii. *Fervour.* You must not go to sleep. You must be all alertness, and have all your wits about you.

iv. *Patience.* You must have great patience, or you will be lost.

v. *Brightness.* You must above everything avoid being dull.

vi. *Humility.* You must never think of displaying your own knowledge, or merely showing off.

vii. *Love.* You must have real love and sympathy with those whom you are teaching.

Catechizing, moreover, requires careful pre-paration. An unprepared catechizing is nerveless, vapid, flabby, and dull, which makes people wonder why it was ever begun, and still more how it ever came to an end, beginning in a haze, and losing itself as water loses itself in the sand.*

* See Canon Randall's Paper on Catechizing read at the Bath Church Congress in 1873.

In the second volume of the Life of the first
Bishop Wilberforce there is an account of a singularly genial, quick, and lively catechizing, which
he himself followed with the greatest interest in
the Cathedral at St. Ouen. "The Abbé," he says,
"was perfectly familiar; sometimes he made the
children smile, then he gathered them up again
into seriousness, and so kept the attention of their
young minds through a good hour. His subject
was " *the nature and attributes of God.*"

'What is God?' he asked. 'A Spirit,' was
the answer.

'Have you a spirit?' 'Yes.'

'What is it?' 'My soul.'

'Did you ever see your soul?' 'Never.'

'Never? Are you sure?' 'Yes. Never.'

'Well then, God too is a spirit. What else
is He?' Then after a pause came an answer—'He
is Perfection.'

'Perfection—what is Perfection?' A longer
pause. At last one replies, 'A quality of goodness.'

'Well, perfection is a quality of goodness
which cannot be better. Let us take one quality.
God is omniscient; He knows everything?' 'Yes,
everything.'

'Yes—all, everything you *say*, but not what
you *think?* When you are set to do some hard
lesson, or to learn some tiresome task, it seems
trying. You *say* nothing, only you think so in your
minds. Your mother does not know that. Do you
mean to say God knows you thought that?' 'Yes,
He does.'

'Oh! But that is impossible.' 'Nay, but He
does.'

'Are you quite sure?' 'Yes.'

'Then if He knows your thoughts, He must be omniscient, and knows all things.' And then he went on to speak of God as the Creator of all things. At the end of the catechizing, they all knelt down, and repeated after him a prayer.*

The who lepassage is worth reading, and illustrates the remark that the secret of success in catechizing lies in "sympathy with children, and a great love for them, for the sake of God Whose children they are." He who believes that children are members of Christ will not measure the responsibility and the privilege of teaching them by the number committed to his charge. He will in this matter of numbers remember the example of his Lord. What a $\kappa\acute{\epsilon}\nu\omega\sigma\iota\varsigma$, what an emptying of Himself it was to go about day after day training that little band of twelve in an obscure corner of a single province of the vast Roman Empire! But with what inexhaustible patience He devoted Himself to their training to be the heralds of His kingdom! But did He not see afterwards "the travail of His soul" and the reward of His labours? There is an account by a leading Indian civilian of a visit he once paid to a very insignificant missionary school at Agra, taught by one then comparatively unknown, though one of the most highly educated Fellows of a distinguished College in the University of Oxford. The civilian magistrate saw the teacher surrounded by some twenty or thirty little Hindu boys. "The weather," he writes, "was hot; the room was small; the subject

* *Life of Bishop Wilberforce*, vol. ii., pp. 289—291.

before the little class was a lesson in Milton's
Paradise Lost. The contrast between the highly
educated teacher and his little dusky flock, between
the sounding phrases of the poet and the Hindu-
stani *patois* of the students, was too great for me.
'Surely,' I exclaimed, as I went out, 'surely this is
a case of labour lost, of talent misapplied, of power
wasted!' But the statesman confessed afterwards
that he was wrong. In six years that little missionary school rivalled the great Government Colleges.
In one of the most thrilling episodes of the Indian
Mutiny the bond of affection between that teacher
and his scholars was of essential service to our
Indian Empire, and there are now in that country
noble types of native Christianity, who owe all they
are to the patient master who in the complete-
ness of his self-surrender thought neither of his
strength nor of his weakness in the discharge of his
self-imposed duty. It is not the number, but the
way the work is done, that decides its efficiency.
The debt we owe to the young is incalculable, for
they will always form a large proportion of our
charge, and their possible influence in the future is
infinite. "I have cause to thank God for your
teaching," a girl said once to her English parish
priest, when she met him in a street of Paris, "for
you bore with me and put the truth before me over
and over again, until even my dull heart came to
understand." She was only one, but who can
estimate the privilege of having brought her to the
knowledge of Him Who in His special commission
to St. Peter bade him not only ποίμαινε τὰ πρόβατά μου,
but also βόσκε τὰ ἀρνία μου?